THE NEW BOSS®

THE NEW BOSS®

The Guide to a Fabulous Lifestyle

Lauren Freeman

TATE PUBLISHING
AND ENTERPRISES, LLC

Published by Tate Publishing & Enterprises, LLC
127 E. Trade Center Terrace | Mustang, Oklahoma 73064 USA
1.888.361.9473 | www.tatepublishing.com

Tate Publishing is committed to excellence in the publishing industry. The company reflects the philosophy established by the founders, based on Psalm 68:11.
"The Lord gave the word and great was the company of those who published it."

Book design copyright © 2016 by Tate Publishing, LLC. All rights reserved.
Cover design by Eileen Cueno and Lauren Freeman
Interior design by Jimmy Sevilleno
Editing by Nicholas Mangieri and Critique Editing Services

Published in the United States of America

ISBN: 978-1-63418-164-8
1. Self-Help / Fashion & Style
2. Self-Help / Motivational & Inspirational
15.11.03

The New Boss: The Guide to a Fabulous Lifestyle is a step-by-step guide on how the dream of being a "Fabulous Woman" can be a reality for *every* woman. By employing "The New Boss Guide Book and Fashion 101 Challenge" as part of this guide book, I will teach *the importance of how a step-by-step makeover will build your confidence.*

My goal for you, is to get on the path to a better life through enhancing your personal understanding of your image, health, and what beauty and The New Boss Lifestyle mean for you personally. Fabulous women, then plan to make changes as needed.

My three "W's" are listed below. This guide book will equip you to move forward.

- *Why*—*I want you to recognize why you must embrace and understand yourself.* Let the past go. You must avoid getting trapped in the past, as it becomes a hindrance to looking fresh and current.

- *Who*—*I want you to learn who you are.* Get a good understanding and true knowledge about yourself, and what suits your own individual personality.

- *When*—*I want you to know when it is okay to let go of things that prevent you from developing and loving yourself.* When you believe in the power of learning, embrace your uniqueness, you will come to the realization that it is okay to focus on being a fabulous woman. "Do You."

If you don't know where to begin, this guide book will serve as your blueprint.

If you put in the time and effort to work on the principles found in this guide book, you will gain or re-gain confidence like never before, as an expression of this, "Fabulous, Healthy, Wealthy, and Think Like A New Boss Lifestyle." Let the transformation begin.

Author LAUREN FREEMAN
The New Boss
DIVA OF DIVAS

Acknowledgments

THIS BOOK WOULD not have been possible without God, who is the best God of all. A special thanks to my father, Willie Frink Jr., and my mother, Loretta Frink, for my humble upbringing. Their support and encouragement, and the way they helped shape and mold me into the woman I am today; I am a reflection of their patience, dedication, and amazing parenting skills. And my reflection of them allows me to acknowledge they are the best parents ever.

I would also like to thank my parents, for giving me a firm foundation to build on; because of my parents, I now live a lifestyle of gratefulness. You are my heart and guiding angels. I have been blessed with two wonderful children. I recognize the love of my son and daughter. Big Boom, my friend and husband, God knew exactly what I needed when He gave you to me. I am blessed to have my family and friends. You all are precious gifts to me. I love Him so much for that. A special thanks to Mr. and Mrs. Steve Harvey, Mrs. Sue Wade, Shirley Strawberry, Johnnie B. Sanders, Dr. Chandra Jones, Nina White, and my professional mentors who have played a role in helping to guide me in the right direction. I love you all like my fabulous pair of shoes.

Finally, a million thank yous to the fabulous team at Tate Publishing and Enterprises. I am honored to be part of your amazing enterprise.

Lauren Freeman's
Autograph Page

"It takes nothing to join the crowd; it takes everything to be fabulous, confident and stand alone."

— Lauren Freeman

To:
_____

From:
_____

"My prayer is that through this guide book, even more people will realize the profound message: It is time for a change, a movement to bring families back to the dining room table, and for all of us to lead by example. In your daily practice, know when to let go and forgive."

Thank you in advance for caring and making the change.

"Anyone can copy or mimic someone else. It takes a real individual; however, to make their own mark in the world. It's called style and Lauren Freeman embodies all that that word means. Her grace, beauty and sheer love for what she does have everything to do with who she is today, a style icon. Thank you, Lauren for using your gifts to selflessly give back and pour into other people's lives. We all look better because of you!"

— Shirley Strawberry

"I could tell you all the things you're expecting to hear about my Mom that she's beautiful, intelligent, independent, successful, influential, etc. I could go on for hours and even though all these things are true; these aren't the only things you should know. My mother is one of the most amazing mom's in the world and I am so happy for her to have completed this book to help other moms and women across the world become successful just like she is. By following along in her footsteps via shadowing both business and fashion wise it has helped me to also grow to be successful and beautiful just like her, and by the time you complete this book I know you will also have the skills to get on her level too."

— Hasani Moussa-Freeman

"This book sketches Lauren's vision of a new global concept of being the "new boss," which means developing yourself to be the best that you have been intended to be. This book incorporates the best of who you are inside and out so that you can improve where you are and establish a legacy of beautifully personification of one's life. Releasing what has been in your heart is not always easy. Sometimes people struggle with the personal issues that have or have not been addressed in their life, and writing a book to the world exposes their good, their bad and their indifference. We spend our lives trying to achieve our purpose that has been instilled in all of us since birth. After talking with Lauren Freeman and reading her book, I was able to discern in her heart the love, warmth, and desire that she has to help bring change to the lives of people. Lauren Freeman has done just that. She has extrapolated the trials and tribulations of her life and has formatted events and life learned experiences into a teaching guide that will improve the life of all who reads and applies the tools and tips for their personal growth. Receiving practical tutelage and tips, you will receive encouragement throughout these pages. All of this information is in one power packed book that is worth the price of admission to a front row seat to a change in your life. Read this book... be open for change. You'll be glad you did."

— Johnnie Sanders

Contents

Foreword

IT GIVES ME tremendous pleasure to introduce and write a foreword for Lauren Freeman. I first met Lauren Freeman at Wade College when she interviewed for the Director position; she came into my office very professional, well-spoken and ready to get to work. Lauren said, and quite boldly might I add, "I would love to work for your college", I could tell right away that she knew what she wanted, and I admired her tenacity and zeal. Although we had no openings at the time, I remembered her when we did and invited her to the President's office for consideration. As I expected, she was hired immediately to work in Wade College's Admissions and Marketing Department. Lauren's personality was a great fit for the position; she relentlessly pursued opportunity, and helped propel Wade College to the forefront of design and merchandising colleges in the metroplex.

While Lauren worked for Wade College, her young daughter would visit the college campus from time to time. While on campus, she would come to my office. To keep her occupied, I would devise various art projects for her. She loved those art projects and always came back for more! Today, that daughter is now a young lady, attending Wade College, which is a testament to the power of purpose. Lauren's purpose at Wade College transcended her own existence, and connected to her daughter's purpose. Lauren has great insight into fashion, beauty and the entertainment industries, and her life is a reflection of that. She went after her dreams, pursued her purpose, and lived life intentionally! In The New Boss, she is sharing real life techniques to help you take control of your life and live your purpose. I watched Lauren day after day, make her own dreams a reality, and I am certain that taking Lauren's advice, and reading this book, will change your lifestyle!

— Ms. Sue Wade,
Founder and Executive Director
Wade College, Dallas Texas

Preface

WELCOME, YOU ARE about to embark on a fabulous journey. Some of you have set out on this journey before, but many of you are going for the very first time. At the end of this fabulous journey, you will arrive at your desired destination. You will have the skills and knowledge, and be equipped to master the mirror. Giving the body the tools it needs is the foundation of self-care, whether your body needs nutrition, movement, sleep, shopping, relaxation, or just a little more fabulous self-love. When reading through these pages, you will get a keen sense of me, from the writer's point of view, and you will feel a part of my work history and gain the knowledge of bringing fashion and health topics together, which we all need to stay on top of, to be the best person that we can be. Keep an open mind to the refreshing instructions and tips on how to improve your current state of being. I will steer away from antiquated traditions and I will provoke your thinking with new thoughts of who you are, and will cause all of us to search deeper for the inner core of our own truth.

"I want to challenge you to know your value; capture your attention with your self assurance, be that self confidant woman. Fall in love with yourself over time as you come to know your own unique look and embrace your fabulous lifestyle. I believe every woman should pledge to first love herself. Know your worth:

"You are far more precious than jewels and your value is far above rubies or pearls" (Proverbs 31:10).

— Lauren Freeman

Why I Wrote This Book

I wrote this guide book with you in mind; I envision your intake of my New Boss guide book as not just reading it and then placing it on a shelf. I wrote this book because there is a big need for a "guide book" as we continue to look at our health, image, and education, we need clear direction and leadership. I want to teach what I wish someone had taught me, continue to help build a healthier, fabulous and respectful relationship with you, and all women across the globe.

There is a need for more role models who are humble. We need more flawless teachers, trained ambassadors, and leadership to teach how to be successful in business utilizing the New Boss guide book. My book can be used by women to coach, empower, lead, and influence other women and young ladies on how to act, and to be, the best role model they can be. I also want women to know our image is not just about clothing; it is so much more.

My book will help you fall in love with yourself, capture the attention of self-worth, build your confidence so you may understand your lifestyle, discover which color looks best on your complexion, understand the importance of your clothing, and that it is a small reflection of your total persona and individuality.

Our image communicates our wealth, health, and lifestyle. I have had to work extremely hard to actually learn and continue to self-manage and change-manage. I beat the odds in the middle of a storm. Most people would crumble from all those expectations and people pulling on them. But I did it with style, panache, and grace, which has led to my overall success. If you have a habit of getting paralyzed mentally when trying to understand your image, health, fashion, and lifestyle, or you can't push past the excuses of not having the right idea of how to move forward in your head, this is the guide book for you.

The additional information in my guide book is an important part of your fabulous journey that follows. References will be made to it. There will be a page for you to add your notes of things that are important to you. I've written this guide book for easy reading, which includes some of my personal experiences and a touch of glamour. The purpose is to share and guide you throughout the book to find what things are particularly relevant to you, what you should know that will enhance the things you already do now: How you look, what you say, how you say it. Through my journey all across the country, I've discovered a demand for personal development (a modern term for polish and fabulous lifestyle).

I will teach you skillful ways to respond to the self-sabotaging thoughts in your mind. You will learn how to focus, set achievable goals, be creative, have fun, be passionate about your journey, and avoid the unhealthy challenges of any shortcomings in your lifestyle, and why you would want to live a stress free, "Fabulous, Healthy, Wealthy, and Think Like A New Boss Lifestyle."

"I love to help; I enjoy giving and making dreams come true."

— Lauren Freeman

I am sharing my master tool, the one I personally used for building a fabulous, successful career for over thirty years mastering the mirror as I did. It starts in the mirror!

Mirror, mirror, on the wall, who is the most fabulous of them all?

Mirror, Mirror, How Do I Look?

Okay, ladies, we need to talk. A strange phenomenon has been reported among women, let's see if you can relate. Have you ever darted from shower to door in two seconds flat, just to get out of the bathroom without catching a glimpse of your body in the mirror? Do you refuse to take the time to embrace yourself? If so, you're not alone. Get a different perspective: This morning when you look in the mirror, ask yourself if you like what you see. Listen to the thoughts running through your mind. Will you look yourself up and down and shake your head in disgust, or will you have a feeling of approval and pride? Write today's date and jot down the answer in your personal study guide.

Mirror of my Mom

Deepest gratitude to my mother, Loretta Frink. I'd like to think that I've mirrored my mom. She was a truly classy woman. I've learned not to be afraid to go bright when everyone else is dressed in black. I believe those who are born with instinctive style are lucky, while others might not be so lucky. Since the very young age of three years old, even then having a sense of beauty and style, I made the discovery of what beauty, fashion, and style are. I know how to choose elegant clothing, superior styles, luxurious fabric, natural fibers like silk, cashmere, and more. I love the fabulous lifestyle of shopping, the art of fashion shows, apparel, accessories, and more. Being a role model for our professional world, my image, years of experience, my eye for detail, passion for beauty, and my love for people just seem to go hand in hand.

"Your future starts today, practice, practice and
great things are going to happen to you!"

— Lauren Freeman

Who Is Lauren Freeman

CEO | PHILANTHROPIST

AN ESTABLISHED BUSINESS leader, entrepreneur, style icon, author, and philanthropist. I come from an extraordinary family, both in size and in accomplishments. My lineage is steeped in entrepreneurship. I am passionate in my quest to challenge my company to positively impact the lives of others. My program is driven to create employment, establish a healthy financial behavior, and improve self-awareness, which will help women lead better lives globally.

By employing a branding and marketing strategy that encompasses various industries, Lauren Fabulous Firm, LLC will equip and engage, while also setting precedents across the fashion, entertainment, and media industries.

With Freeman at the helm of Lauren Fabulous Firm, LLC, all endeavors are poised to exceed industry standards. Freeman's experience, which spans from the fashion and entertainment industries to the marketing and public relations industries, will contribute to the positioning strategy of Lauren Fabulous Firm, LLC. In addition to her extensive experience, Lauren Freeman is on track to receive an honorary Doctorate degree in Public Relations.

Introduction

How to Score Lauren's Fabulous Lifestyle

I AM OFTEN asked for a simple, effective, no-nonsense approach to the above comment about how to attain my personal lifestyle. It starts with the mirror and I score high with goal setting. I will share how that can be used by anyone, anywhere, and anytime. It is a simple process that is easy to learn, easy to apply, and easy to get results and score big.

Whether you realize it or not, you are being judged by four things:

- *What you do*
- *What you say*
- *How you look*
- *How you think*

Women, young and not-so-young, realize they feel insecure in too many important areas and wish for the information that will help them put their best self forward. You might be thinking right now, "*Yes, that's me. I do feel a little or **very** insecure about myself.*" And you're not alone!

Even at the literate school, Oxford University, a survey showed that almost all of the students reported some uncertain feelings about how to dress and how to act, and about 10 percent reported great difficulties in many social situations. In my guide book, there are several essential components I will address, starting with a thirteen-step makeover on goal setting and planning. I will explain the importance of shared success and how it depends on each woman's fundamental commitment to results and accountability, and recognizing the competencies required to be successful. Using the thirteen-step makeover, you will achieve positive results on your specific goals in order to keep your lifestyle balanced. Information on how to grow, mirroring knowledgeable selective information based on your fabulous goals is included. I encourage a daily practice and applying the new approaches to your polished lifestyle. This will include how to dress for success, steps for interviewing, planning, goal setting, why it will influence what you do, how you look, what you say, and how you say it… for the rest of your life! So, it's pretty commonly accepted that change is a fact of life and even change is changing all the time.

Self-Managed: A Mindful Lifestyle

Mindful ladies, I'm so happy you're on board; the fact that you're reading these words lets me know that you are like me. You want to be a self-managed woman who makes positive behavioral changes by choice, and you want to create a well-balanced environment and surround yourself with a healthy lifestyle. But we can't do it on our own. We have our strengths, to be sure; but we also have our weaknesses. We all make mistakes. We all need help!

You can either help, or harm, your efforts to begin thinking in a healthy way. In order to change your behavior, take a good look at how your mind may be standing in the way of change. Before we begin to identify and help you understand the importance of how to think and self-manage your image, a gift we all can relate to, you must learn how to manage your image and lifestyle. Exactly what is it that you are trying to deal with? What changes have influenced your mental lifestyle? What role do you play? What responsibilities are exclusively yours? Do you know your gift? Are you owning it? As we begin to understand what it takes to master the gift, and why we need to know our role, it is imperative that we understand the difference between thinking about mastering our gift, and actually MASTERING our gift.

Can you continue to live in the present moment? Will this be the year for you to master your gift, the year of a mindful living that will shape the life you desire and beyond?

"Master your gift that's been designed by God... exclusively for you, celebrate every day and enjoy each moment of your life."

— Lauren Freeman

The Importance of Fashion 101

Why is Fashion 101 so important? What will I learn? What is it all about? After surveying and teaching many women well over thirty years throughout my career, what I've found is that there's a demand for Fashion 101 in our lifestyle. The guide book will teach you how to identify your image using the mirror signature tool, how to use a clothing guide, accessories guide, where to shop, what to buy, gain the power to love the new fabulous, flawless you, and more. Personalize your guide book as we start to create your image journey, then on to the next steps of doing you! Please keep in mind why you want to follow the signature mirror instructions, and practice daily using the mirror to influence your belief in the new self-managed you. For effective results use it on a daily basis. *Without a mirror, can you see your image?*

> *"Girls of all kinds can be beautiful—from the thin, plus-sized, short, very tall, ebony to porcelain-skinned; the quirky, clumsy, shy, outgoing and all in between. It's not easy though because many people still put beauty into a confining, narrow box...Think outside of the box...Pledge that you will look in the mirror and find the unique beauty in you."*
>
> —Tyra Banks

1

Who Are You?

Circle below to identify who you are

- **Elegant Women:** *Elegant women, like to be stylish and elegant. They like their clothes to be formal and in top form. They do like the fabric to be the best, with elegant, monochromatic colors. Two colors may often be the limit in an outfit, rather than the commotion of too much distraction in their look. Elegant people like their clothes in superior styles and quality, which conveys enrichment, formality, and wealth. To have developed the style of elegance in a person, they are probably now in their mid-thirties or forties. Women of this style convey the look of authority, executive and corporate. They love luxurious fabrics and natural fibers like silk and cashmere.*

- **Classic Women:** *Classic women, their look is timeless, with out-fits that are not extreme in fashion. Their clothes are tai-*

lored and semi-fitted from top to bottom. Classic styles are very versatile and functional. With natural colors in the fabric, they add dominant and bright colors for accenting. They are at their best in matte surface and traditional prints. They do not like anything extreme.

- **Diva Women:** *Diva women, do not judge themselves regardless of what mistakes they might make. They know that aiming for perfection is really failure, because it is just a way to beat yourself up inside. Moreover, because of these attributes, a diva woman can handle all social situations and conversation with confidence.*

- **Glamour Women:** *Glamour woman, God equipped her with beauty and class. They have been conditioned to accept less and less in the name of glamour and beauty, but to them, less is not more. More is more. They are beautiful inside and out. They don't socialize with everyone, but are kind to everyone. The glamorous person does not like anything fake.*

- **Feminine Women:** *Feminine women, mastering the feminine look requires elements which are draped and softly structured, in a modest length with small details, and soft-textured fabrics. Feminine women love their natural fiber with matte-sheen in light to medium colors and prints. The feminine person is romantic and captivating. The look they convey is relaxed, gentle, and caring. They appreciate the fine things in life, like soft and luxurious clothing. They like taking life easy and don't like to be hurried. In business attire, the feminine woman will find it difficult to convey the look of authority, because of her soft nature. The feminine style in shoes is medium to high.*

- **Creative Women:** *Creative women, are so unique, you can't copy the way they dress even if you tried. They are artistic and very creative. They can actually pull together a completely distinct look by mixing different styles or colors, and actually succeed. They love accessories in any size and weight, any unusual* shape. *They are not afraid to show their body piercing, daring and bright-colored hosiery.*

- **Modern Women:** *Modern woman, certainly is fashionable, very colorful, lots of high heels in every color. Price is of importance. They like very nice looking skirts, long to the knee, combined with a beautiful shirt, which they often put inside the skirt. If a modern woman can only afford one or two pieces, it would be tailored pants, dress and jacket that are form-fitting.*

- **Sexy Women:** *Sexy women, are glamorous, seductive, and feminine. Sexy people could be very curvy or slender in body form. The look gives one message, and the message is exciting and compelling to men. This dress form is sexy and provocative. No element of classic in the construction of sexy clothes. These are tight and body hugging and show a trendy hemline, short or long. The look is both in bold and daring or basic colors. The fabrics worn often have glitter and shine into them. Many are in animal prints with low-cut tops.*

- **Natural Women:** *Natural women, love to wear clothes that are natural and casual in style, and still give them comfort. These gently tailored clothes are easy to care for, usually in medium to light colors, and practical in style and look. The fabric is made from natural fibers in matte finish and practical in length. Often they are in unmatched pieces with no visible coordination. They love the look of sporty patterns that are structured like menswear.*

- **Dramatic Women:** *Dramatic women, love their look in clothing. Her clothes are always highly structured with lots of dramatic lines and designs. She prefers big bold prints with lots of colors, crisp fabrics in geometric and abstract designs, and lots of patterns. Dramatic women like to be noticed and be the center of attention. They give the air of authority and convey confidence in their unique look. They like to be in control in any situation. Their clothes reflect their personality, the look* *of strength, and authority in style and color. They like to be around people with energy and excitements. Their heels are medium to high.*

- **High Quality Women:** *High quality woman, is a woman of value. A woman who values the happiness of others, and who is considerate. People will rarely perceive real value in you unless you give them something. Tailored dresses and pants in your wardrobe are form-fitting, well-made, and good quality. Another feature of the high quality woman is the fashionable shoe. High heels are high quality. Respectable and lovely, a genuine, feminine woman, holds and thinks of herself highly, regardless of what life circumstances may present, and despite what other people may think.*

- **Low Quality Women:** *Low quality woman, places low value on herself and has such a low sense of self-worth that it's impossible for her to perceive what life is like from another angle. She's too into herself! It's very much a case of "the empty vessel makes the most noise." Usually; this kind of woman is so significance-driven that she is habitually unable to listen, care for, or help others. Typically, this kind of woman makes you cringe, because she gives the female gender a bad name. She may even frustrate you with anger because you simply can't get a word in, and let's face it, it's hard being around someone who doesn't care about you at all.*

- **Trashy Women:** *Trashy woman, is someone who is constantly sucking value from others. No support, just empty, viewing life as a playground rather than a battleground, and looking for evidence to support that belief of negative judgments. Crying over a tragedy (being lied to by a man or something) and all the girls are saying, "Don't worry, honey, you can get anyone you want, he's just a slag." Well, this is mostly useless because most women in this situation don't make any changes and just proceed to think trash.*

- ***Respected Women:*** *Respected women, probably one of the most important attributes a respected woman has is a great smile, great attitude, and great posture. She's neither glamorous nor elegant. She knows the importance of great posture and that it affects how others perceive her a lot more than one could imagine. As humans, we are all drawn to people or things that seem to be of high value, and to humans who project themselves as high value.*

The Traits of a Woman: Woman, female, lady. These are nouns referring to adult human beings who are biologically female. A wealthy woman, a strong woman, a woman with character, a woman of unbridled appetites, a God-fearing woman, a refined, polite woman, is a real lady in all things and behaves like a lady.

Woman Defined

Was "taken out of man" (Gen. 2:23) and therefore the man has the preeminence. "The head of the woman is the man;" but yet honor is to be shown to the wife," as unto the weaker vessel" (1 Cor. 11:3, 8, 9; 1 Pet. 3:7). Several women are mentioned in Scripture as having been endowed with prophetic gifts, as Miriam (Ex. 15:20), Deborah (Judg. 4:4, 5), Huldah (2 Kings 22:14), Noadiah (Neh. 6:14), Anna (Luke 2:36, 37) and the daughters of Philip the evangelist (Acts 21:8, 9). Women are forbidden to teach publicly (1 Cor. 14:34, 35; 1 Tim. 2:11, 12). Among the Hebrews, it devolved upon women to prepare the meals for the household (Gen. 18:6; 2 Sam. 13:8), to attend to the work of spinning (Ex. 35:26; Prov. 31:19) and making clothes (1 Sam. 2:19; Prov. 31:21), to bring water from the well (Gen. 24:15; 1 Sam. 9:11) and to care for the flocks (Gen. 29:6; Ex. 2:16). The word "woman," as used in Matt. 15:28, John 2:4 and 20:13, 15, implies tenderness and courtesy and not disrespect. "Only where revelation is known has woman her due place of honor assigned to her." (*Easton's 1897 Bible Dictionary*)

Getting Started

Sit in front of your favorite mirror or favorite place, and start your search in the mirror. Once you identify who you are, let's learn and plan how to fix our weaknesses, and use our inner strength to own our image and style. Stretch and grow as individuals. Know that someday, with practice, you can style yourself more consciously, hold yourself accountable and focus on the new, fabulous woman that you are. The good news for us is that many women have been successful using parts, or all of this approach! I'm elated to share my journey with the mirror throughout my career. I too, used the mirror as one of the ways to become more confident, mirroring success. I know how it works; you must believe, because our beliefs will have a profound impact on how successful we are.

Throughout the guide book you will learn to think like a new boss, how to use the skills of mastering the signature tool called mirror. This is part of your new, fabulous, healthy, and wealthy journey and destination. Look at how our beliefs influence our actions, our health, and our lifestyle. Can we influence ourselves to be happier, healthier, more fabulous? Can you give thirty minutes per day to practice the beliefs of your fabulous lifestyle journey?

What do you believe?

- *Religious beliefs influence the way you behave*
- *Religion affects all your thoughts and beliefs*
- *Political beliefs and genetic makeup can influence your belief*
- *Religion can influence political beliefs*
- *Perception can influence our beliefs*
- *Beliefs can influence and change your relationships*
- *Beliefs create and influence reality*
- *Your family influences you*

- *You can influence your dream*

- *Your mom can influence you*

- *Your health can influence and affect you*

When I was a little girl, my father would say to me, "Listen up, my child. If you don't know where you're going, you might end up somewhere else." He also said, "You must always know where you are going."

I can truly say I know where I'm going as my father said to me. Do you know where you're going?

"Think like a new boss and live a
fabulous lifestyle every day, over time."

—Lauren Freeman

Your Personal Study Guide Notes:

_____

_____

_____

_____

_____

_____

_____

_____

_____

_____

_____

_____

_____

_____

_____

_____

_____

_____

_____

_____

_____

_____

2

Thirteen-Step Makeover

WHAT FOLLOWS IS what I affectionately call, the thirteen-step makeover. Follow it to the letter and you will be quite pleased with the outcome. Continue to use these steps for each additional goals.

1. *What specific goal do you want to achieve? Write it down.*
   Be precise or don't bother moving to the next step.

2. *Why must this goal be achieved now?*
   Be clear on the key drivers and motivation, or the first obstacle will be your undoing.

3. *Who will help you to achieve this goal?*
   Be sure these are the right people, with the right talents, attitudes, and intentions.

4. *Where do you currently stand in relation to this goal?*
   Deal with the facts and identify the size of the performance gap.

5. *How do you plan on accomplishing this goal?*
   Be deliberate. Identify the exact steps, tasks, deadlines, and assign responsibility.

6. *When will victory be claimed for belief and action?*
   Be committed, believe, enforce your deadline, and focus on the goal until achieved.

7. *Search for and apply a number of simple, yet highly effective strategies for a lifestyle change. Starting today, focus and get fired up.*

8. *Imagine the difference in your life if you could read or display your perfect life.*
   Close your eyes, dream, plan a more fulfilled, healthy financial behavior; live your God-chosen life.

9. *Create strong solutions to tough problems.*
   Be aggressive. Prepare to move quickly and decisively.

10. *Dig deep and display confidence you can feel and others will believe. Make it drama free with a twist of elegance. It will change your life and give others hope for their future.*

11. *Find solutions that are flexible and offer a personal approach to a fabulous, confident, and more self-managed you.*
    Realize and mirror that you are very special and there is only one you.

12. *Exemplify excellence in your daily image through dedication and hard work.*
    Salute the most important player—fabulous you.

13. *Write the process for doing something you always dreamed of doing to make a difference.*

Congratulations for being fabulous and committed to being the best new boss!

"We are not born with these qualities; they are learned."

— Lauren Freeman

Your Personal Study Guide Notes:

_____

_____

_____

_____

_____

_____

_____

_____

_____

_____

_____

_____

_____

_____

_____

_____

_____

_____

_____

_____

_____

_____

_____

_____

_____

3

Why Fashion 101

Fashion 101

A FEW YEARS ago, I thought, what if I could create a transformational learning solution: One platform, multiple solutions that could create fabulous transformations in any woman's life. No matter what situation they live in, no matter what beliefs they hold, no matter what dreams they have, career or not.

Platform Fashion 101 is my way of helping people create and develop a new look through the knowledge gained by my experiences. I am excited to share why Fashion 101 makes sense and how it works. Using this technique, "Team" Fashion 101 and I, will analyze and do a makeover on you in the comfort of your own home. We will help you build up your wardrobe, focus on getting new pieces to pair, utilizing your existing pieces. Fashion 101, includes a closet makeover. We will identify the clothes which best fit and flatter you, and help you avoid those impulse purchases that end up as costly mistakes. We will also show you how to use accessories, mix and match outfits to achieve different looks, thus enabling you to maximize every single item in your wardrobe and leaving you with a shopping list to follow up on as you wish.

You will learn

Fashion Basic 101

- *Your personal style*
- *Your best colors*
- *Your body shape*
- *Your face shape*
- *What to wear and how to wear it*
- *Wardrobe essentials*
- *Closet organizing*
- *Outfit ideas*

Style Guide 101

- *What's fabulous*
- *What's chic*
- *What's business casual*
- *What's formal after five*
- *Fashion inspiration for all sizes*
- *Fashion vintage*
- *Fashion Bohemian*
- *Fashion global*
- *Street eco-friendly clothing*

Clothing Guide 101

- *Fashion tops*
- *Dress shirts*
- *Sweaters*
- *Denim jeans*
- *Pants*
- *Jackets*
- *Coats*
- *Dresses*
- *Skirts*
- *Body shapers*
- *Beach and swimwear*
- *Petite fashion*
- *Plus-size fashion*
- *Discount clothing*

Accessories Guide 101

- *Handbags*
- *Purses*
- *Shoes*
- *Belts*
- *Scarves*
- *Hats and caps*
- *Hosiery*
- *Fine jewelry*

- *Fashion jewelry*
- *Sunglasses*
- *Headbands*

Private Shopping 101

Includes initial consultation, visualization to discuss your shopping needs, body shape, budget, and lifestyle. We will visit selected boutiques that are going to work for you, because we have already identified the ones that will be most appropriate. Our focus will be given to those shops which can deliver your style. Fashion 101 will provide a list and advice on how each item works for your individual shape, color palette, and style. We'll put together unique outfits that can be used with your existing wardrobe. Whether you're looking to spend half a day or a full day, my team and I will take care of your personal shopping needs and make shopping a fabulous experience! Or feel free to consult with us, if you feel unsure or need additional help at any point.

> *"Shopping is golden when you know your budget,*
> *style and your fabulous body shape."*
>
> — Lauren Freeman

Your Personal Study Guide Notes:

_____

_____

_____

_____

_____

_____

_____

_____

_____

_____

_____

_____

_____

_____

_____

_____

_____

_____

_____

_____

_____

_____

_____

_____

4

Development of a
Fabulous Woman

The Development of a Woman

MOST EVERY PLACE you go, there is at least one lady who is the big "attention getter." She is attractive, and as you look closer, you notice the attention-getter smiles a lot and has warm personal charm.

Although a closer look reveals that she's probably not the classic beauty, there is something uniquely beautiful about this woman. What holds your attention is her confidence and the attention she gives to those around her. She has a gift for focusing on others and making them feel special.

She knows what to do, how to look, what to say, and how to say it. Good news. The attributes the "attention getter" possesses can be yours. Good grooming, great posture, a warm smile and soft eyes, good manners, a sweet personality, and wholesome character. These are qualities you can have for the time it takes to do a little reading, practicing, and studying.

Visual Poise

What is an attractive girl's most valuable asset? Is it her expensive clothes? Her clever use of accessories? Her tasteful application of makeup? No!

A women's most valuable asset is beautiful carriage. Good posture! Good posture is "the proud look" the hallmark of a woman. The insignia of nobility. You can spend hours perfecting your hair, makeup and clothing, but it will be a wasted effort if you don't know how to handle your body.

Body Language

The way you stand and move is body language at its most basic. It gives out a subliminal message to the world that you are insignificant, timid and unattractive. If you are proud of yourself and the way you look, almost automatically that pride is revealed in your carriage.

Good Posture

Growing up in a family of thirteen was not easy when it came to our parents. My parents did not play, they would demand that we sit up and stop slouching, for no other reason than it might make us look bad. I'm so happy to say it's more than looking bad, there are so many other elements to the importance of posture, elements that are affecting millions of us every day.

From neck and back pain to blood flow and respiration, posture can have a major impact on how we live and how we feel every day. It can actually amplify beauty and even help create it for plain women. Without it you're only half the woman you can be. You will feel confident when you move with poise and efficiency. Once you know the simple elements of good posture, it's easy to achieve a beautiful and fabulous you.

For best posture practice, do these three movements: Roll your shoulders down and back then pull your elbows back toward your back pants pockets (this presses your scapula up against your ribs, as though you were using them to push your heart up and out).

Beauty

On special nights, allow yourself to sit down in front of a mirror and actually take time to savor the ritual of beauty.

Skin Product Tools

Once you have achieved radiant skin, take a large brush for a more natural application and brush a matte bronzer where the sun would hit the face. Run the bronzer along the jawbone to make the face look less full and to disguise jowls and any hint of a double chin. Then add a pop of cream blush in the apple of your cheeks. This gives a natural, stained-glass window effect, like you are blushing from the inside out.

Lip Color

Great skin with a healthy pop of color must be paired with some full, pouty lips. Full lips are a psychological marker of attraction for men. They make you look younger and balance the symmetry of the face. If you don't have Angelina's pout, you can get it. There are hundreds of great lip-pumpers on the market. But first, take a few seconds to make your lips kissable, take your pointer finger and tap briskly on your lips. This brings circulation and blood to the area. Then apply your plumper for instant fullness. Finally, top those kissable lips with a sheer nude-pinkish gloss.

This makes the lips look moist, healthy and youthful. For beautiful lip maintenance, I suggest you run your toothbrush across your lips after you brush your teeth. This removes dead skin for soft lips. Always apply lip moisturizer or Vaseline on lips at night before bed. And I *must* remind you, don't smoke!

Eyes

For eyes, brush a neutral, matte, fleshy color all over the lid. This, paired with a soft eyeliner kept close to the base of the lashes, is often enough. The important details about the eyes that will truly change the way you look are the eyebrows and lashes. Eyebrows are more important than hair when it comes to a woman's beauty.

Basic Steps

These are basic steps which should remain consistent in your routine. Remember: Flawless, radiant skin; healthy color in the cheeks; a soft kiss of the sun; full pouty lips; strong, perfect brows; great, big, fat lashes; and a subtle glow. You will always look healthy, polished and pulled together. Makeup is an amazing tool, but you hold the power to transform not just the way you look, but also the way you feel. There is nothing more beautiful than a woman who looks life in the face and sees it's magic. Confidence and comfort in your own skin is the best beauty secret. So, if you feel overwhelmed by makeup and the process of reinventing yourself, learn it. Knowledge is power. Read, practice, and even take a private makeup lesson.

Good Grooming

Being well groomed is a matter of becoming organized. It's a way of life, making certain that you look fabulous and put together. To become meticulous and polished requires no more than setting up a beauty routine and sticking to it. You do some things every day and others every week. Once you are well established in your routine, you will meet the world polished, confident, feeling fabulous and with everything going for you.

Fabulous Beauty Bath

A bath can be a powerful sedative for your nerves or it can be wonderfully rejuvenating. To enjoy the perfect bath, choose a time that's convenient for your family, as well as yourself, so you won't feel rushed. Shampoo your hair and massage the conditioner into your head and scalp. Wrap your wet head in a towel, getting the hair out of the way. Climb into a tub of warm water, bubble bath and relax for a while.

- *Lather your body with your favorite soap until the bubbles grow.*
- *Next, a good brushing on the finger and toenails.*
- *Now shave away the fuzz from under your arms and legs.*
- *Rinse soap away with fresh water.*
- *Step out of the tub and dry yourself.*
- *Give yourself a good rubdown with a nice body lotion and dust with a fragrant bath powder.*
- *Apply deodorant, face moisturizer, and style your hair.*

Manicure

Lovely hands are manicured regularly. If your hands are dry or in bad condition, apply a soothing, rich lotion or petroleum jelly at bedtime, and sleep with your hands in cotton gloves. Apply a rich hand cream, oil, or lotion every time you wash your hands and go all the way to the elbows. Keep all nails the same length, medium to short. Well-cared-for nails and hands make you look feminine and pampered. A word of caution, polish looks pretty only when it's perfect! Be sure to remove the polish at the first sign of chipping.

Pedicure

Follow the exact same procedure as the manicure, except cut toenails short and straight across. Toenails must be meticulously groomed. If you wear sandals (and if you wear hosiery), keep your toenails shorter than your toes. Lovely feet are done regularly. Treat yourself to a professional manicure and pedicure once or twice a month. You'll love it and you're worth it!

Eyebrows

Eyebrows are incredible! Their shape can influence the way you look and how people react to you. Eyebrows create the framework for the eyes! The eye is just a picture until you frame it. Clean foundation out of eyebrows, use an eyebrow brush or an old toothbrush, and brush the brow upward. Be certain you shape the brows well by tweezing stray hairs. If your brows are well shaped, you may find they look best natural, with no pencil. Do not color in your eyebrow as though you were drawing on canvas, if your brows are pale or uneven, use a pencil and make short and feathery strokes to fill in the brow.

Eyebrow Color

Eyebrow color, if used, should be applied in short, feathery strokes, and then brushed to avoid a harsh line. It's not a good idea to use black brow color for sketching brows, it's too harsh for most women. Check the shape of your brows in the mirror with a critical eye. Watch for shapes that are quizzical, mean, dragon-lady like, or eternally surprised.

Eyebrow Threading

Eyebrow threading is a practice of shaping the eyebrows using cotton thread. The twisting action of the thread traps the hair and lifts it out of the follicle. It's a very gentle, sanitary, and painless way of removing unwanted facial hair. Threading is also used to remove hair from the upper and lower lip, as well as other areas of the face. This method of hair removal is more effective and less painful than tweezing and waxing, and is a good alternative to waxing and tweezing, especially for sensitive skin.

Why is threading better than waxing or tweezing?

Overall, threading is the inexpensive and effective method of hair removal, without the increased chances of wrinkles and peeled skin, unlike waxing. It also is an excellent option for those women who cannot wax. Threading is more precise and the hair grows back finer and slower. There is no burning, peeling, or irritation and a great remedy for ingrown hair.

Eyelashes

Lashes are important to your overall look. They bring the eyes up for an instant lift. Make sure you have great mascara in your makeup bag. Apply a few coats of mascara followed by a lash curler.

Teeth

Keep them clean! Brush after every meal and snack, if possible. Brush up and down and not sideways. Place bristles slightly under the gums. Be sure the toothbrush bristles are not too stiff, brush tongue and gums thoroughly, rinse with mouthwash, floss at least three times a day, and purchase a new toothbrush every three months. Don't bite metal objects or pull on things with your teeth. It's easier than you think to break a tooth. See your dentist twice a year.

Face

Even if you don't feel like you have the looks of a millionaire, put your millionaire smile on. It goes a long way and brightens your face! Using a little makeup really makes a difference. The three essentials I would recommend are mascara, lipstick (or a great lip gloss), and some blush. This will add color to your face and make your features pop. I have never bought into the notion that designer or expensive makeup is best. I've used mainstream brands and organic/natural makeup my whole life and have always had compliments. These products are a quarter the price of department store brands and you can buy them anywhere. The key is to keep the makeup simple and light. Don't wear heavy foundation and loose powers with bright lipstick and heavy eyeliner. Remove hair from your face.

A basic element of physical attractiveness is, first, great skin with a glow. Everyone can get it! This glow imparts radiance, a healthy youthfulness to the skin. You can achieve it a couple of ways. I believe beauty is a whole process and what happens inside often tells the story outside. So, drink plenty of water. Skin that is dehydrated looks tired, old and dull. Sip white-tipped tea and green teas. These are packed with antioxidants, which give a beautiful glow from inside. As far as skin care goes, you must exfoliate. This is like polishing your skin. It removes dead skin cells so light can hit all the smooth places of your face. Finally, a sheer foundation that boasts the ability to produce radiance should look natural and elegant with the right shade and application of blush and lipstick, and a black/brown or black shade of mascara. Spend less money on makeup, but spend more time on mirroring and mastering a natural look to give you radiance.

Hair

Keep hair clean, medium length, and a color found in nature. If God wanted you to have purple hair, he would have made you an eggplant. Also hair that is teased "high and wide" has negative class connotations. Buzz cut is open to too much interpretation. Unless, of course it's a "trendy" work atmosphere. In that case, it's a plus. Come to think of it, purple hair might also be a plus in this situation. The bottom line for the more traditional office is to keep your hair tasteful and conservative. Besides, the hair spray needed to maintain a highly teased style is murder on the ozone. Groom your hair neatly. Tone down the "big hair" on your head.

Tips

Good grooming builds self-confidence. Everyone responds favorably to a well-groomed fabulous woman. Search magazines and newspapers for articles on grooming, find pictures of well-groomed women, and find pictures of unkempt individuals.

- *Good grooming keeps you looking healthy and attractive.*
- *Good grooming increases your chances of getting the job you want.*
- *Successful women and girls need to know that good grooming is essential to getting ahead in a competitive world.*

Back Proper Posture (Neutral Spine)

Improper posture may put too much stress on your back and neck. The key to good back posture is to keep the right amount of curve in your lower back. A healthy back has three natural front-to-back curves that give the spine an "S" shape. Too much curve (swayback) or too little curve (flat back) can result in problems.

The right amount of curve is called the neutral position. Having good posture helps maintain the natural curves of the back and keeps it strong.

- *Take a picture. Print photos of proper posture and put them up where you can see them easily and even set a timer to be reminded every twenty to thirty minutes to correct your posture. In time, this will become automatic and you will self correct with very little effort.*

- *See a professional, such as a chiropractor or physical therapist. See someone who specializes in improving posture using a proven science-based approach. In my experience, everyone is a unique case, and if you are having posture issues or chronic pain, improving your posture can be a life-changing gift.*

- *Use props and tools. Tools, such as lumbar support pillows and seat wedges, help maintain normal spinal curves when sitting to decrease posture stress.*

- *Wear posture-enhancing shirts and sports bras. These support proper posture and cue your posture muscles to engage, while training your upper back and core muscles to become stronger and more posture fit.*

Proper Sitting

Slouching puts stress on your lower back and contributes to low back problems. When you sit, keep your shoulders back and down, chin back, belly in and your lower back supported. Your spine should be in the neutral position, with three general front-to-back curves. Use proper sitting posture. If your chair doesn't give enough support, use a small pillow or rolled towel to support your lower back.

- ***Sitting and working at a computer:*** *Our bodies are designed for movement, not sitting for long periods of time.*

- *Talking on the phone, texting, etc.:* Most folks tilt their head while talking on the phone, or slouch the head forward while texting.

- *Tight front of the body:* We all need to focus on opening and lengthening our front, while performing exercises and movements that strengthen our back. So treat yourself more like an athlete, and less as a desk jockey.

- *Slouching while driving, flying, or taking the train:* Studies show that the vibration created by engines can oscillate at a frequency that relaxes and sedates your muscles, so your body is in a poor position, and your muscles have to work even harder to support you.

- *Stand on your entire foot:* Most people stand with weight over their heels, causing the feet to become weak and turn in, which increases stress on the weight-bearing joints (ankles, knees, hips and lower back).

- *Whether standing or sitting:* Become ergonomically sound with your computer setup. Keep your eyes level with the top of monitor, elbows and wrists straight at 90-degree angles.

- *Move often and use all of your motion:* Try every day to play with the kids, your pets, or even play around in your garden. Remember to never bend over, but instead hinge from your hips.

- *Get a TRX or suspension strap:* Put it up in a spot where you walk often during the day. Use it frequently to stretch and open up your tight muscles. You can also do pulls and rows for your shoulder blades when you use a suspension strap.

Lifestyle

Inner Beauty

Using dream coaching, Emotional Freedom Technique (EFT), and numerology will work on bringing out the inner beauty that may be lying dormant due to past traumas, toxic relationships, or childhood beliefs that are preventing you from living a fabulous life on purpose. Beauty is all about perspective.

Be Beautiful Now

Whether it's healthy and glowing skin you are looking for or learning from a professional about makeup application, skin care treatments, detoxification, or beauty applications; the result is you looking beautiful and feeling fabulous.

*"Nothing makes a woman more beautiful
than the belief that she is beautiful."*

— Sophia Loren

Style: A Way of Life

Now let's talk about the parts of our lives that may be a little more personal than everything else. Our style determines how we make our homes, relate to our loved ones, raise our children, save our energy and manage our health, setting goals, planning, balance over all the well-being of those around us, a manner of living that reflects the person's values, attitudes, and lifestyle. If you like your list of goals, stick to them, because sometimes we can set goals and attempt to achieve too many. It's the worst thing you can do if you're trying to transform your life and have a balanced fabulous lifestyle. Mirror the lifestyle you desire and dream of, make your plans in your personal study guide notes **designed by you**; your choice, your lifestyle, starting with our list below.

- *Fashion*
- *Manner*
- *Mode*
- *Style*
- *Attitudes*
- *Habits, or possessions*
- *Fashionable or desirable lifestyle*
- *Luxurious semirural manner of living*
- *Fast lane*
- *Free living*
- *Vanity fair*
- *Salaries*
- *Pharmacology designed to treat problems, such as impotence or excess weight, which affect a person's quality of life rather than his or her health.*

Planning and Management

What is the importance of planning and management? Planning is the first step and the most important function of management. It is needed at every level of our lives. Planning reduces risks of uncertainty. Future activities are planned in order to achieve objectives. It reduces overlapping and wasteful time. Planning promotes innovative ideas. Clear planning selects the best alternative out of the many available. One of the most important things to remember to wear is your smile! Walk confidently and have a positive attitude.

Time Management

How do I get a lot accomplished each day? The solution I learned is to stay focused on the priority of tasks and plan to accomplish them in order of importance. It helps to plan, using a checklist, and mark things off. This really works and keeps me on task. Keep in mind, planning is the most important part of the formula we call time management. Some of you say, "I don't have time to do any planning," or "Things change too much to plan!" Research shows that for every one minute you spend in planning, you will gain ten in execution. One minute equals ten minutes. Ten minutes equals an hour and forty minutes! This may seem amazing because you feel like you are already doing all you can each day! If you could just gain an extra half hour a day through effective time management, you would have twenty-two more days available to you per year.

Time Planning

Planning will keep you on course in achieving your goals and objectives. You have to take time to make time. Planning is the difference between being *reactive* and *proactive*. When you don't plan, you end up responding to the day's events as they occur. Learning to manage your time better, will free up time to do the really important things. Great rewards come from good time management habits.

What does a reactive day look like? You arrive at work in the morning with no clear idea about the day's activities. The morning mail arrives, the phone rings, people drop by with various requests. You do your best to respond to these various demands. You put forth considerable efforts, but at the end of the day, you haven't accomplished anything significant. Be proactive. Plan and work your plan daily.

When urgent things happen, you usually react to them. But you must be proactive, rather than reactive, to do the important but not so urgent things. Only by saying no to the unimportant can you say yes to the important. If you neglect prevention and planning, crises will own your life. If you plan daily instead of monthly and weekly, you will live in the urgent, where your "planning" will only prioritize your problems. If you don't, there is a severe danger that trivial, time-consuming activities of the day, will push the critical few entirely off the calendar.

Remember, there will always be more things to do than time to do them. Sometimes you must forget something you would like to do, in favor of something that has to be done, to accomplish your objectives. Don't fail to plan. If you do, plan to fail.

Healthy Lifestyle

Healthy lifestyles play a major part of your life. How are you living your life today? How do you desire to live? Do you dream of a healthy lifestyle? You decide. Okay, let's take a closer look at your health. Take a deep breath in, slowly breathe out, smile, say, "I love some me!" Keep your head up. Remember, there's only one fabulous better you. You will need to use your personal study guide notes for this section.

Stand in front of your mirror and answer these four health-related questions. Take as much time you need.

1. *Are you healthy?*

2. *Do you have a good health plan?*

3. *Do you know how to be healthy?*

4. *Are you willing to change what you see and mirror a healthy lifestyle?*

Are you looking for a healthy life? Look no longer, it begins on your knees or on your back, whatever it takes to get an understanding of the above questions and your answers. It begins in your heart, when that little girl inside you opens the door so the light can stream in. Tell him, "Here's the truth, God, I love bad food and I don't know why. I have health problems but I don't know why. I diet and I don't know why. I count calories and I don't know why. I'm overweight and I don't why."

Your heart needs to get in line with what you write down and see in the mirror. He will not force you to accept, live an abundant and meaningful life that he has in store for those who believe in him. That is your free will, your lifestyle choice.

When I think how can I explain why a healthy lifestyle is so important to me, I remember the time I lost someone so dear to me, and many others we cannot have back on this earth. It hurts my heart when I see women who I can touch and who are still on this earth breathing and can make this lifestyle change. So here you are. Go. This is for my mom and you. I choose this lifestyle. The path of Christ has made all the difference for me. When we root ourselves in him, his path leads to a fruitful life. My life is not perfect and that is a promise to no woman. But instead, it is a fruitful life. When I think about Thanksgiving, not only do I think about my mother, my father and family, how she made sure that this day was celebrated, all your favorite food, fruit, vegetables, turkey, stuffing, dressing specially prepared with the unconditional love of a mother of thirteen, I also think about those who don't have, and I pray for them all.

I'm forever grateful to have abundance and this is what I have in my life today.

So much for that, let's get back on track. Write your healthy lifestyle answers in your personal study guide notes. In your guide book, follow the makeover steps and start your daily healthy lifestyle management plan. Use the guide book and check with your experts that specialize in getting you to a better, healthier life. I hope this helps, and I want you to know that, I know how hard it is. Of course, understanding and better planning, staying focused toward your mirrored plan and goals will get you to the healthy lifestyle! I've been there, helping and supporting women for over thirty years. Personally, I am not going to argue with the Creator of the universe about a better way. I have made too many mistakes to tell him that my way is better. He always makes me better for having fallen. That's the beauty of the narrow path. He's there to pick you up and dust you off when you fall. Practice and practice more. I love it!

We can have the best career, home, family, and money. I believe our health and a healthy lifestyle should be number one on our New Boss list. Physical, healthy living to me, must include a balance in all aspects of health—physical, spiritual, mental, emotional, environmental, and social—to promote a healthy lifestyle. This is a way of living happily, while practicing good eating and exercise habits, combined with a healthy belief system, which brings comfort to whatever it is, from polytheism to atheism, so long as it makes you happy.

I like the definition of health as given by the World Health Organization: "Dynamic, ever-changing process of trying to achieve your individual potential in the physical, social, emotional, intellectual, spiritual and environmental dimensions."

Why should you be drinking water?

I am sure most people know that, drinking water is deemed to be a healthy thing. However, the UK as a nation is a population of dehydrated people. http://www.patient.co.uk/doctor/acute-kidney-injury-pro.

We fall short of the recommended eight glasses of water a day. Many people claim that water tastes boring and instead opt for a sugary drink, which is not benefitting their waistline or their health.

Today, I want to study some of the benefits of drinking water, in the hope that some people may adopt adding water into their daily routine. Water has so many health benefits. It really can help you lose weight and to feel more energized. Your body is comprised of 60 to 70 percent water, and as such needs water to keep your body functioning at its optimum. Drinking plenty of water flushes toxins and ensures that your cells get all of the oxygen they need to function as they were meant to.

Ten Benefits of Water

- *Your brain consists of 90 percent water so if it is 2 percent dehydrated, it has a 20 percent knock on effect of making you feel fatigued, lacking in concentration and even experiencing headaches and migraines.*

- *Water can help your mood and help with the symptoms of depression.*

- *Your blood consists of 83 percent water and it is your body's transport system, distributing essential nutrients around the body.*

- *Water assists digestion, absorption and assimilation of food. You need to drink enough water to get the full benefits of the nutrients that you eat.*

- *Water will protect and moisturize your joints by keeping the cartilage soft and hydrated.*

- *Water moisturizes the air in your lungs and can protect your lungs from the buildup of mucus.*

- *Water will regulate your body. If you don't drink enough water, you will compromise the evaporation process that your skin uses to keep you cool.*

- *Water assists excretion of waste from your bowels and your kidneys. Being dehydrated will mean that you will become constipated and put your kidneys under stress.*

- *Water allows your kidneys to remove toxins from your body. It allows your cells to take in nutrients and it also allows them to expel waste products. If you don't drink enough water, toxins will build up, weakening your immune system.*

- *Your muscles consist of 75 percent water so water can help you maintain proper muscle tone by giving them the natural ability to contract and not be dehydrated.*

- *One of the most overlooked factors in exercise is adequate water consumption.*

- *This should be a no-brainer since water comprises up to 70 percent of the body and if you're dehydrated; your muscle size suffers as well.*

- *When your body doesn't get enough water, it begins to dry out. The skin and hair are the first and most noticeable areas of dryness from dehydration.*

- *Water helps to reduce blood pressure.*

- *When you do not drink adequate amounts of water, the body will compensate by retaining sodium. That should be a red flag. Sodium is directly related to high blood pressure.*

- *Water improves skin and hair. Drinking water will promote healthier scalp and healthier hair.*

Think of a plant which is not watered very often. Does it thrive and look healthy? Of course, the answer is no. Your hair and skin are the same, and need to be well nourished with a healthy diet and lots of fresh water. Plants can easily revive and flourish once the dead leaves are removed; the plant is given the essential nutrients and well watered. So the same applies to our skin and hair. Exfoliate your skin, have a good haircut and then start to add in the water that your body needs and see the difference in a matter of weeks. Oh, and just to repeat, drinking the right amount of water can help you lose weight, which is obviously a huge plus too.

So I hope you can see that it would benefit you to drink the correct amount of water every day!

Your Personal Study Guide Notes:

_____

_____

_____

_____

_____

_____

_____

_____

_____

_____

_____

_____

_____

_____

_____

_____

_____

_____

_____

_____

_____

_____

_____

_____

_____

Dress for Success

MY EXPERIENCE FOR over thirty years as a career woman, dressing for success and teaching women in the corporate world how to dress for success and more, there is so much to know, however, we've turned the corner. It's a level playing field in the corporate world and equity abounds as it relates to women. This is partially true. The chapter, Dress for Success, will give instructions on wardrobe, fashion design, image restyling, tailoring services, teach women how to dress for success, and show ways for you as a woman to ensure you get the utmost consideration and respect in your endeavor(s).

Instructions

The first rule of thumb in dressing for success is to not wear pants. Pants are okay to wear at work or during other activities outside of work, but when you're looking for the promotion or next step in your career (success mode), think custom tailoring. Conservative companies wear dresses, tops and skirts. Have integrity. Be confident in who you are.

Dress for Success

Do not be suggestive in your dress wear. The old "if you got it flaunt it" attitude will cause you to fail or not be taken seriously. Wear skirts or suits when you are in success mode. Choose colors like charcoal, gray, or dark blue. Wear high quality black or brown shoes. Make sure your shoes are closed toe and closed heels.

Fashion Communicates

It tells a story as effectively as words. The old saying "You can't judge a book by its cover" doesn't hold true for people. How you look says plenty about how you see yourself and how you want others to see you. The way you dress, how you cut your hair, wear makeup and jewelry, others will interpret these details as signals, which they use to inform themselves about you.

A few things that can backfire on you include visible body piercings, visible tattoos, tight clothing etc. These things can send the wrong message. Stick with things that are mainstream and conservative when you are in success mode.

Don't try to look like anyone else. Be the best you. Develop an upright professional posture when walking, standing or sitting. Exude total confidence. My life, my choices, my mistakes, my lessons, and my business. Minding your business comes with a lot of humbleness and respect for others, and again not everyone does that. So, let's learn together how to mind our own business and stop poking our nose everywhere.

In all my growing years, I have come across various people who lack the quality of humbleness. And I have noted these people are somehow obsessed with boasting, and also a hint of low self-esteem. Why do you need to be so loud when making a point so that the whole room notices you, and not just the person you are talking to? Or why do they need to say sentences like, "Why are you wearing this dress?" If the difference of opinion comes from someone you love, a little adjustment and some compromises can easily solve this problem. Moreover, respecting the other person's opinion will always take a relationship a little further. But if it is with someone you don't care about that much, why bother? Who cares about what other people think when you are happy with yourself? Everybody's philosophy of life is different. To live in harmony and not make enemies, one has to be modest and respect others. Knowing to mind your own business will always earn you respect and your own personal space in exchange.

First impression is guided by your appearance. Fashion is body language and clothes are the vocabulary. Consider the fact that each day for 365 days a year you put on some combination of clothing. Are you confident about the choices you make and comfortable when wearing them?

Buying Process

I strongly recommend you put thought and care into your buying and selecting process, as this is directly linked to the message you send out. Use the style guide and mirror to build your personal style, know your values, gain a better understanding of your personal lifestyle. How does the influence of the media play in your lifestyle? Are your individual interests, activities, physical geographic environment, and balanced lifestyle affected?

Personal Style

I believe a woman needs, and should have, her own personal style; to flatter her physical shape age, and to mirror and reflect her own unique beauty and personality through individual beauty. If you dress yourself, learn the rules, dress for the occasion, don't wear black every day, wear appropriate hemlines, invest in your hair, shoes, perfume, and makeup. Do you, the correct and polished way!

Care for Clothes

One of the major factors in my career that I have learned, is understanding how to keep my clothes looking fresh and new with my business and personal attire. I learned by checking them often and giving them good care. That way, I could always maintain that fabulous look. You want to inspect your clothes for loose buttons, frayed hems, spots, and broken threads before you return them to the closet. Mend these immediately and then hang them up for wearing. Keep a small sewing kit in your closet. Remember which garments must be dry cleaned. Check your clothes every weekend for items that need to be pressed or go to the cleaners. I use padded hangers to keep the shoulders from stretching and dropping, if you do not have the correct hangers, you may want to fold your sweaters and knits, and place them in a drawer or on a shelf. Place perfumed sachets in drawers with socks, hose, panties, slips, and bras. Always check your shoes after each wearing for dust and mud. From years of experience, I recommend polishing your shoes that you wear often every week or more if needed, have run-down heels repaired, store shoes with a shoe tree. Also, put baking soda on the closet shelf. It helps to keep the closet smelling fresh.

Avoid packing too many clothes in your closet. A good rule is if you have not worn it in the last year, you probably will not wear it again. So avoid clutteritis of the closet and share your used clothing with thread swapping (read more about thread swapping and membership in chapter 16 and chapter 17).

Tips

A well-organized closet can save you searching time and effort and gives you that wonderful, organized, "I've got it together" feeling. Closets and drawers are a great place to start organizing a lifestyle of good grooming. When you are organized, you feel good and fabulous.

Business Professional Company

Guidelines for Business Professional

When you are dressed in business professional attire, your clothes will look nice on you, because they fit well and you look like they belong to you. Good quality, custom design from beginning to end. Every detail selected by you, well-constructed clothes are a good place to put your money options, business, formal, and casual. High quality, manufacturer designed, ultimately will fit well and laundry or wash well. Keep in mind to choose clothes you can move around in.

The navy suit should be your first suit. Next, there are nine more suits essential to a complete professional wardrobe. These include glen plaid or navy windowpane style, the Birdseye style (which is a weave that looks solid from afar but has a subtle texture up close), and the lightweight tan suit, ideal for spring and summer meetings. The charcoal gray solid looks great for inter-company meetings, second interviews or meeting clients, who will feel more comfortable with someone dressed in gray. Down the road, you'll be able to invest in more interesting styles, such as a light-gray ensemble. Dove-colored version is great for summer. Two-button blazer and wool-crepe trouser has a light, fluid shape, ideal for warm days, and the straight-leg trouser hits just above the hip. What's more, the lining stretches with the fabric so you can move comfortably.

If you're worried about how you're going to afford ten suits don't. Start off slowly and build up a collection, paycheck by paycheck. As long as you have two to four good suits in rotation, your clothes should remain looking fresh.

The simple ones will be just fine. The simpler they are the longer they will stay fashionable, and the more fashionable they make you look. Buy an "easy" fit, clothes that are not too tight or skimpy and not too large and baggy. Choose professional clothes with simple lines and you can change the way they look with jackets, sweaters, scarves and belts.

Buy separates, blouses, shirts, sweaters, turtlenecks, skirts, and pants that will stretch your professional wardrobe. Buy your separates with a color plan in mind so you can mix and match easily. Today, shoppers have plenty of freedom in colors and exciting accessories.

- *Brown, then buy your separates in brown, beige, rust, coral, gold, tan champagne, amber and ivory.*

- *Navy or maroon, then buy your separates in navy, maroon, pale blue, all shades of gray, slate blue, emerald green, red, and gold.*

- *Red and navy, then buy your separates in red, navy, bright green, pale blue, white, wine, slate blue, and all shades of gray.*

Business Casual Company

Guidelines for Business Casual

The business casual wardrobe has always been important to professional success. Without a doubt, it's more critical and important than ever. A competitive business climate means you have to stand out. Many companies that went "business casual" are haywire. People are showing up dressed for nightlife or soccer games, not for the office and in doing so, they are losing their professional edge. I get so many complaints about the way people dress for work. With that in mind, I wrote this chapter to give more of a guide on how to dress and more, as a successful businesswoman. Throughout my career, I've always taken care of our home and our children, yet still made time to always look professional and current. I love to wear a piece of clothing with very strong and fresh colors. From time to time, I find inspiration in colors that make me look like a perfect businesswoman. Read more about some creative ideas on how to make fabulous, fresh colors out of your business combinations. Classic trousers and jackets are basic features of the modern businesswoman. They can give you a classic glamour, elegance, and add color to your outfit.

Certainly, wear a very nice looking skirt, long to the knee, combined with a beautiful shirt which you can put inside the skirt. Other features of the modern businesswoman are fashionable shoes and high heels. Heels can be semi-high or can be low and not in strong colors. The difference between a classical outfit and everyday outfit, is that classical clothing is more severe and does not allow for playing with many colorful and extra fine details. Look at this inspiring collection of great combinations of modern businesswoman magazines.

- *Your business casual wardrobe should consist of the same type of clothes and accessories described in your organization's dress code.*

- *If your company does not have a documented business casual code, emulate the dress of the person whose position you want!*

- *Business casual does not give you license to wear short skirts.*

- *Business casual may mean a blazer and skirt.*

- *Wear skin-toned hosiery when your business outfit consists of a short-sleeved jacket or dress.*

- *The best guide is to tune in to the dress of those moving up the corporate ladder.*

- *Dress for the position you want, not the position you have.*

- *Wear shoes that are well maintained.*

- *Press your clothing; you are what you wear.*

Keep a "business professional" outfit at the office for emergencies.

The Perfect Business Casual Looks

Capsule Wardrobe

Conservative Company

Guidelines for Business Conservative

- *Your attire at a less conservative company may mean wearing a light sweater or knit top worn under a blazer with a skirt or slacks.*

- *A colorful blouse will look beautiful with any of the cutting-edge skinny jeans, leggings and boot-cut trousers. Summer to fall graphic patterns and sultry solids are perfect for mixing and matching. For fabulous chic sophistication, the tweed sweater jacket is your go-to item.*

- *Accessorizing the conservative look is of the utmost importance. Accessorizing can bring a whole new look to clothes. The look in clothes brings in a new look. Accessories worn, the shoes, hosiery, all the little things like jewelry, bags, belts, scarves, new ideas spring up to give apparel a new look. The*

*look is current hit, fashionable way of dressing in a conserva-
tive company. It's something you want to "be with" every season. It carries over in popularity to the next season.*

- *For casual Fridays, I suggest wearing a suit the first week of
work so you can gauge how others in the office dress. They may
allow khakis—and maybe even denim. Pair them with a
simple navy blazer and penny loafers, but if you have a pen-
chant for dresses, a casual shift works with a cardigan draped
over the shoulders, worn with either pumps or sandals. If you
go with the latter, make sure your company doesn't have a
policy prohibiting open-toed shoes.*

- *Achieved through stark lines and color combinations, ruffles
will sway you toward a more feminine style, be it a single
wave on a structured silhouette or grand with tiers and tiers
of it. If ruffles are too flirty or soft for your style, the le smoking
(the tuxedo) returns, in proportions that are anywhere from
rigid to oversized and boxy, in classic black wool or in lux
silk should you be inclined to show some skin without looking
too revealing.*

- *Tribal trimmings make it a ritual to combine artisanal fringe,
wild prints, and dramatic patterns. Cropped trousers cut with
a slim-fitting silhouette and a shorter inseam lengthens the
legs and creates a taller appearance. Shimmer and shine, no
longer relegated to evening metallic, add a glamorous accent
for day and full-on for night. The jumpsuit, not just for the
Studio 54 set anymore, streamlines the silhouette and creates a
long and lean look.*

Dos and Don'ts

- *Long fingernails, especially with bright or specialty polishes.*
- *Short-sleeved shirts, even worse, open-sleeve shirt or blouse.*
- *Fishnets, patterned hosiery or bare legs (no matter how tan
you are).*

- *Socks that don't match your shoes or socks that are too short.*

- *Don't wear hosiery and shoes that are darker than your hem.*

- *Don't wear belts and shoes that don't match.*

- *Rumpled or stained clothing.*

- *Scuffed or inappropriate footwear, including sneakers, stilettos, open-toed shoes and sandals.*

- *Strong perfumes (Many people are allergic to certain scents).*

- *Don't wear slacks to work if you've never seen top-level women at your organization wear them.*

- *Remove all tags and extra buttons and remember to cut off the zigzag thread that keeps pockets and slits closed.*

Undergarments

Many women focus on their outer wardrobe and forget what is hiding underneath. It is important to frequently wash your bras as well as camisoles, etc., on the delicate cycle. It is very unappealing to see a well-dressed woman with a frayed, dirty bra strap peeking out of her top. Likewise, underwear and socks need to be replaced when stained, start to look thin or have holes or elastic coming apart. This is not sexy for your partner or for yourself! You can typically buy a bunch of inexpensive clearance rack panties that look like all styles. You'll pay around two to five dollars per pair and they look great! If they get ruined in the washing machine or wear with time, you can just toss them without thinking twice. While we are on the subject, ladies, do buy bras that fit your cup and your body properly, and are seamless. For bra size and bra calculator, see an expert at Victoria's Secret or your nearest department stores. Bras aren't meant to cut into your skin and cause a ripple effect. There is nothing worse than a great top with seam lines, back fat, or nipples showing!

Your Personal Study Guide Notes:

_____

_____

_____

_____

_____

_____

_____

_____

_____

_____

_____

_____

_____

_____

_____

_____

_____

_____

_____

_____

_____

_____

_____

6

Interviewing

What to Wear in an Interview—Top 13

1. *Skirt suits in dark colors, i.e., black, navy, or charcoal gray.*

2. *Blouses should be simple in style, in a white or soft color.*

3. *Stockings that match your skin tone.*

4. *Your wardrobe reflects who you are. Don't let it say the wrong things.*

5. *Suit, blazer with a skirt or dress (should be conservative and below knee length).*

6. *In a recent study, 90 percent of college recruiters agreed pants suits for women are acceptable.*

7. *Wear shoes that are well maintained.*

8. *Press your clothing.*

9. *Wear one pair of simple earrings.*

10. *Shoes should be pumps or medium heels.*

11. *Purses should be medium or small. Make sure it matches your outfit.*

12. *One ring is most appropriate.*

13. *Briefcase should be well maintained.*

How to Dress for a Job Interview

Perfect grooming is your first assignment when you interview for a job, whether you want to be a CEO or an entry-level factory worker. To a prospective employer, how you dress says a great deal about you.

Things You'll Need

- *Hosiery*
- *Silk Scarf*
- *Skirts*
- *Turtlenecks*
- *Women's Blazers*
- *Women's closed-toed shoes*
- *Women's Dress Coats*
- *Women's Dress Pants*
- *Women's Dress Shirts*
- *Women's Suits*
- *Sweaters, Vests*

Best Colors to Wear

What you choose to wear on an interview communicates a lot about who you are and how you see yourself, so in the all-important job interview, what color should you wear to make a great first impression? Of course, blue and black are the best colors to wear for a job interview, and orange is the worst. Conservative colors, such as black, blue, gray, and brown, seem to be the safest. Navy blue is one of my favorite colors to wear on a job interview, because it exudes trust and confidence. You are more likely to get the job when you wear navy blue to an interview.

- *Black—Leadership*
- *Blue—Team Player*
- *Gray—Logical/Analytical*
- *White—Organized*
- *Brown—Dependable*
- *Red—Power*
- *Green, Yellow, Orange and Purple—Creative*

Interview Process

- *As you walk to the door, remember your visual poise.*
- *Make eye contact.*
- *Position yourself before speaking, relax, and take a few calm seconds to arrange your notes. Smile, look up and speak.*
- *When you have finished your last word, make eye contact.*
- *Stand, shake hands, step back, turn calmly with your head up.*

Invited to Enter Interview

- *Knock at closed door and wait until you are invited to enter.*

- *Stand quietly until she or he speaks to you.*

- *Do not stand in a doorway and block the flow of traffic.*

- *Wait your turn to go through a door.*

- *Kindly thank anyone who opens a door for you.*

- *As you enter a job interviewer's office, hold your purse and resume in one hand and open door quietly with the other hand.*

- *Step inside and quietly close the door with the same hand.*

- *Wait until you are invited to be seated before seating yourself.*

- *When you leave the interviewer's office, stand, shake hands and thank the person.*

- *As you are saying good-bye, maintain eye contact as you move toward the door.*

- *Try not to turn your back on the interviewer as you exit the door, especially if either of you are speaking.*

- *Close the door quietly.*

Tips and Planning

- *Call the receptionist or secretary at the prospective employer's office for tips on what employees there wear.*

- *Consider the job's location. If it's a library in a strip mall, you can wear a sweater and slacks. At a corporate office, wear a conservative business suit. A pant suit with a sweater or blouse is appropriate for an informal office.*

First Impressions

About 75 percent of the decision to hire is based on the applicant's appearance. Within the first thirty seconds of an encounter, eleven assumptions, including credibility, are made about the person being presented. Though it may seem unfair, evidence like this demonstrates your image alone has the potential to project your level of professionalism, which can make or break your credibility. "In social or business settings, clothing acts as a communicator of us, our company, and our position." Clothing alone can communicate respect, authority, position, and credibility. The way in which we use it affects the way others respond to us.

- *You have one chance to make a first impression. It is better to dress too formally than to dress too casually.*

- *Trendy is fine, as long as you keep your style subtle. Clothes make a strong statement about you. What do you want to say?*

- *Wear a silk scarf and carry a nice briefcase or portfolio. Leave the oversized, disorganized handbags at home.*

- *Avoid mini skirts, tight sweaters, sloppy overalls, and sandals with straps.*

- *Closed-toed shoes, pumps and loafers. If you are wearing a skirt, nylons are a must.*

- *Tone down the use of makeup, hair spray, perfume, and jewelry. One nose ring is one too many, and may cost you the job of your dreams.*

- *Inspect your hair, nails, hems, and the shine on your shoes.*

If Interviewing Late in the Day

- *Brush hair and teeth*
- *Check footwear for scuffs*
- *Check your outfit for holes, tears, stains, or winkles*

Interview Tips

Role play with someone else or in front of a mirror. Come prepared with stories that relate to the skills the employer wants, while emphasizing your:

- *Strengths*
- *Willingness to work and flexibility*
- *Leadership skills*
- *Ability and willingness to learn new things*
- *Contributions to the organizations in which you have worked or volunteered*
- *Creativity in solving problems and working with people*

List Questions to Ask at the Interview

Pick questions that will demonstrate your interest in the job and the company. This might include commenting on the news you learned from the company website and then asking a question related to it. Also, ask questions about the job you will be expected to perform.

- *What are the day-to-day responsibilities of this job?*
- *How will my responsibilities and performance be measured and by whom?*
- *Could you explain your organizational structure?*
- *What computer equipment and software do you use?*
- *What is the organization's plan for the next five years?*

Be Prepared

Remember to bring important items to the interview.

- *Notebook and pen.*
- *Extra copies of your resume and a list of references.*
- *Copies of letter(s) of recommendation, licenses, transcripts, etc.*
- *Portfolio of work samples.*

On the day of the interview, remember to plan your schedule so you arrive ten to fifteen minutes early. Go by yourself.

- *Look professional. Dress in a manner appropriate to the job.*
- *Leave your coffee, soda, music, headphones, and backpack, at home or in your car.*
- *Turn off your cell phone.*
- *Bring your sense of humor and smile.*

Be Confident

Display confidence during the interview. Be confident, but let the interviewer start the dialogue. Send a positive message with your body language.

- *Shake hands firmly but only if a hand is offered to you first.*
- *Maintain eye contact.*
- *Listen carefully. Welcome all questions, even the difficult ones, with a smile.*
- *Give honest, direct answers.*
- *Develop answers in your head before you respond. If you don't understand a question, ask for it to be repeated or clarified. You don't have to rush, but you don't want to appear indecisive.*

End with a Good Impression

A positive end to the interview is another way to ensure your success.

- *Be courteous and allow the interview to end on time.*

- *Restate any strengths and experiences that you might not have emphasized earlier.*

- *Mention a particular accomplishment or activity that fits the job.*

- *If you want the job, say so!*

- *Find out if there will be additional interviews.*

- *Ask when the employer plans to make a decision.*

- *Indicate a time when you may contact the employer to learn of the decision.*

- *Don't forget to send a thank-you note or letter after the interview.*

Women Entering the Workplace

- *How you dress.*

- *Your handshake.*

- *The biggest nonverbal cues.*

- *Your wardrobe reflects who you are. Don't let it say the wrong things.*

- *No matter what you wear, be professional.*

- *Your attitude should reflect your ambition.*

Success Starts With You!

- *Listen attentively when others are speaking.*

- *Make an effort to be on time.*

- *Make promises and keep them. Say what you will do and do what you say.*

- *Ask intelligent questions.*

- *Take pride in your appearance at all times.*

- *Smile more often than frown. It takes three muscles to smile and fourteen muscles to frown. Why strain yourself?*

- *Work hard, be dependable, don't be an excuse-maker.*

- *Quickly acknowledge all gifts and kindnesses extended to you.*

Reasons People Don't Get Hired

- *Application form or resume is incomplete or sloppy.*

- *Overly aggressive behavior.*

- *Lack of maturity.*

- *Lack of interest and enthusiasm.*

- *Nervousness or lack of confidence and poise.*

- *Responding vaguely to questions.*

- *No genuine interest in the company or job.*

- *Lack of planning for career. No purpose and no goals.*

- *Overemphasis on money.*

- *Unwillingness to start at the bottom.*

- *Negative attitude about past employers.*

- *Failure to express appreciation for interviewer's time.*

Hired or Not, You Should Know

I believe you would want to know when an interviewer decides whether or not you are a bonafide candidate for the job. When they read your resume? When they are dazzled by your intelligence? Nope. It's when you walk through the door.

Avoid discussing personalities and taking part in criticisms and arguments. Keep your speaking voice soft, clear, and well modulated. Make an effort to understand others' viewpoints, even when they do not agree with yours. Don't offer too much advice or be an excuse maker. Being careless about your grooming, using poor grammar, bragging on yourself and your accomplishments, giving information that is not entirely correct, and speaking as though you know the whole truth, these things should also not be done.

Stop being mad if someone does a job better than you!

Understanding

Many leaders mistakenly believe people have bought into the vision when they understand and agree with it. However, being convinced is not the same as being committed—it's only the initial stage. I can think of dozens of causes I know all about and greatly admire, but to which I am not committed or even remotely connected.

Commitment to a common cause develops through a series of stages. Only when the final stage has been reached does a person fully "buy in" to the leader's vision.

Share This With Your Friends!

How to Get a Promotion

Do you feel like you're stuck in your current job? Are you ready to move up? It's tough to climb the corporate ladder, but if you want a job that excites you and pays well, you'll likely have to make the climb at some point. If you want to get a promotion, you'll need to be a patient team player, while also being an ambitious self-promoter. It's a difficult balance to strike, but these tips can help.

Work for a company that can give you room to grow

The type of company you work for can determine your potential for promotion. When applying for jobs, seek out companies with opportunity for advancement. You don't have to work for a huge corporation, although these usually offer plenty of promotion possibilities at any given time, but you do want to look for a company that has enough going on, so you can be assured you're not running into a dead end. Preferably this company will be doing well and growing, though many companies, especially very large ones, tend to grow in cycles.

Concentrate on just doing the best you possibly can in your current position

Excellent performance reviews aren't sufficient to get you a promotion, but they are necessary for it. So are good attendance, punctuality and a willingness to go the extra mile when the company needs it. Showing up five minutes early and leaving five minutes after your shift, can turn into a fortune of extra income over your lifetime, when you are the one who gets the promotion.

Make sure people know you're doing a great job

You don't want to toot your own horn too much, but you can't always expect your merits to speak for themselves. Keep in good contact with your supervisor and make sure he or she knows what you've been up to (assuming you've had some smashing successes). Don't be an attention grabber or "brown-nose," but make sure people know who you are and make sure you get credit where credit is due.

Be popular

In an ideal world, promotions would be based solely on merit. We don't live in an ideal world though, and office politics will often play a role in who gets promoted and who doesn't. Use and develop your people skills. Be kind and helpful to your coworkers, supervisors, and underlings. Develop relationships with people you work with, play golf with the boss, and get to know people (other than your immediate supervisor) who make decisions in the company. Be present at company events and network with people from outside your department.

Make sure the right people know you want a promotion

Don't be afraid to tell your supervisor about your career goals. Most good supervisors will ask you about them and try to be helpful. Continue to do a great job in your current position and don't seem fed up with your current work, but let decision makers know if you really want a particular job.

Apply for jobs within the company

These days, you cannot just wait for a promotion to fall in your lap. That happens sometimes, but most promotions, especially at large companies, require you to go through the application and interview process, and usually you'll have to compete with candidates from outside the company.

Apply for the right positions

Don't just apply for any opportunity that pays a bit more than your current job. Look for opportunities you are genuinely interested in and you are qualified for. You don't have to have all the skills listed in the job description and you probably won't, but you want to be able to make a good case that you'll be able to get up to speed quickly.

Take the application process seriously

Too often, internal candidates figure they've got the new job in the bag, but studies show that as few as one-third of internal candidates win the better jobs they seek. External candidates can be extremely competitive because they have no pretenses of security, they want the job and they know they'll have to put their best foot forward to get it. In addition, companies sometimes want to bring in new people to bring new skills or perspectives to the organization. The lesson here is don't be complacent, and remember to "sell" yourself as you would if you were applying for any other job.

Seek out new skills

If you become the best customer service representative of all time, you're well on your way... to remaining a highly regarded customer service representative for the rest of your career. It's not enough to be great at your job, you also have to develop marketable skills that prepare you for more responsibility. When you gain skills and qualifications far beyond what your current job requires, your employer may see keeping you in that job as a waste of your talents.

If you have earned a Bachelor's, consider earning a Master's or PhD

But only if one of these qualifications will help you achieve your career goals. Don't just go back to school for the heck of it. Instead, think about what programs will help you climb the corporate ladder. Sometimes specialized professional designations or licenses can be far more important to getting a promotion than degrees, and sometimes you may just need to take some classes to improve your computer skills or accounting ability, for example. There are a wide range of education programs available that allow you to go to class in the evenings or on weekends, and there are also ample opportunities for accredited self-study and online learning. What's more, your employer may reimburse you for certain tuition expenses, so it may be possible for you to expand your knowledge at no cost to yourself.

Learn a second/third language

Due to the increasing globalization of the world in general, more and more companies will be looking for people who know multiple languages. Learning more than one language also means you don't need a translator, which opens up international positions (such as a manager for an entire continent, as opposed to a state or small country).

Take on temporary projects

Temporary projects can be a great way to broaden your skills and network with people from other areas of the company. Many people feel uncomfortable volunteering for these assignments because they can be challenging and force you out of your comfort zone. That's the point.

Volunteer

If you are not getting new skills at work, consider volunteering your spare time to a nonprofit organization. Large, well-recognized nonprofits almost always offer a wealth of opportunities to learn new things, and smaller organizations may also have suitable projects you could work on. Successful nonprofits typically look to fill volunteer positions with people who are qualified to do the job, but with a little persistence you should be able to find an opportunity that uses your existing skills, and helps you build new skills. Your community involvement can also be a plus toward you getting your promotion.

Get a mentor

A strong relationship with a manager or someone higher-up in your department can open a lot of doors for you. For one thing, you'll likely learn a lot about the organization and about the jobs you might want to get in the future. For another, you'll have an ally who will be willing to go to bat for you when you do decide to apply for a new opportunity. Finally, your mentor may groom you to succeed him or her when they move up or retire.

Groom a successor

It's a common paradox: You're so good at your job that you're indispensable, but you're so indispensable in your current position that the company would fall apart if you were to leave that position. The solution to this problem is to take another employee under your wing and train him or her so that they will be ready to fill your shoes if you get promoted. Some people are afraid that their understudy will take their job if they do this, but as long as you're a great employee and continue to develop your skills, the only way you'll lose your current job is by getting promoted. Training another employee (or several) also shows you have management skills and you care about helping other employees develop their skills.

Develop a new position

If you figure out a better way to do your existing job or see the need for a new position, don't be afraid to talk to management about creating this position. Since you're the one who saw the need and presumably, you're best qualified for the position, this can help you take on new responsibilities, even if you don't get a big pay raise at first.

Seek employment elsewhere

If, for whatever reason, you seem to be at a dead end with your current employer, it's time to look for better opportunities elsewhere. This can be hard if you feel a loyalty to your employer, but you need to do what is in the best interest of your career, or you will become unhappy with your job. Recent surveys show that as many as 75 percent of employees are looking for new jobs at any given time, so you won't be alone.

Remember

We don't win by accident. We simply cannot rely just on talent to take us to the top. Winners display strong, durable commitment, both to a common cause and to others. This commitment inspires us to persevere through setbacks and to make the sacrifices necessary to succeed!

The Price of Top Talent

Median income for Americans was $34,750 in 2012. At some companies, however, the median is more than four times as much. Based on figures provided by the careers website Glassdoor, 24/7 Wall St. examined the highest-paying companies in America.

The companies that pay their employees the most fall primarily into two industries: Management consulting firms and tech companies. These companies employ graduates of elite schools whose skills are in high demand and have high salary expectations to match.

Consultancies can afford to pay high salaries. Generally, they are high-margin businesses, relying on a relatively small workforce to generate revenues. For tech companies, maintaining the talent pool requires paying very high salaries to bring in the best software developers and engineers.

Many of the companies paying the highest salaries are head-quartered in some of the wealthiest metro areas in the country. Boston, the fifth-wealthiest metro area by median income, is home to the second-highest paying company. San Francisco, the nation's fourth-wealthiest such area, is home to four of the top payers.

But no metro area is home to more top-paying companies than the San Jose area, which topped the nation with a median household income of $79,841 in 2012.

To identify the companies paying employees the most, 24/7 Wall St. reviewed data from Glassdoor on median annual salaries by company, as well as job reviews and average salaries for specific positions.

We also examined Glassdoor's 2014 study on the Best Places to Work. In addition, we reviewed 2012 median salaries by occupation from the Bureau of Labor Statistics (BLS).

- *24/7 Wall St. to see five more*
- *Average Wall Street Bonus up 15% in 2013*
- *10 Companies Paying Americans the Least*
- *9 Cities Where Wealth is Soaring*
- *America's Most Content and Most Miserable States*

Your Personal Study Guide Notes:

_____

_____

_____

_____

_____

_____

_____

_____

_____

_____

_____

_____

_____

_____

_____

_____

_____

_____

_____

_____

_____

_____

_____

_____

7

Professional Appearance

P ROFESSIONAL APPEARANCE SHOULD suggest your preparedness for different situations, the importance you place on your job, and the respect you have for yourself and others. Clothing that is low quality or inappropriate, demonstrates carelessness for your appearance, and a lack of respect for the impact you have on your company, which leads people to question how much value you really place on your job. Keep your clothing updated, making sure you have classic pieces, comfortable fits and year-round fabrics to get the most mileage and confidence out of your closet.

This goes without saying, you have to dress the part of the professional to be a professional. No one has ever advanced at work or preserved their job by dressing like a slob. There is no advantage to dressing in an unflattering way. Humans are primarily visual creatures so you have to appeal to this faculty as much as possible. Wearing decent clothes is easy, just do it! It just might save you or boost your reputation. It is the ultimate professional accessory.

Keep good basics in your wardrobe that are truly timeless and will last the test of time and fashion trends. Key basics include black dress pants, have about three good quality pairs. You will want at least one pair to have a pin stripe which will give your body some length and add variety, as well as one pair with a cuff on the bottom, and one without. All pairs should have a crease running down the leg for that dressy look. Avoid anything with pleats which are currently outdated and tend to make you appear larger in the front.

Do invest in good quality tops, such as short sleeved and three-fourth-length tops with Lycra (to keep their shape) in both V-neck and round neck styles. I recommend black, white, and red. If you cannot wear red, perhaps gray. Under blazers with pants can also be worn with jeans on a casual Friday. You will need about three nice black skirts, a pencil skirt or slight A-line, one with a tasteful print, and one that is more airy, flowing, and fun. Dress shirts for women are more popular than ever. You will want to have some variety here. I recommend buying shirts that fit your shoulders and arm length properly, and have a bit of Lycra or stretch fabric so you can move freely. Make sure the buttons across the chest don't gape open. These can be bought anywhere such as Boutique Stores, T.J.Maxx, or department stores. Keep winter and summer colors separate.

Bargain Professional Classy Look

For some women, the concept of dressing classy without spending a lot of money seems impossible. An inexpensive garment is possible as long as it is fitted to suit your body, and can give you a more expensive, designer label look. Many equate designer clothing and accessories with the look of class. You can still achieve the wardrobe you see in magazines and on the runway without emptying your wallet. It is a great feeling to get a bargain when an item looks much richer than what the price tag indicates.

Here are some simple tips to achieve a grown woman look, whether you're heading to the office, gym or for a night on the town.

The Classic Style

Mastering the classic look is having timeless outfits that are not extreme in fashion. They are tailored and semi-fitted so you can actually dress down or up. Classic styles are very versatile and functional. In color and fabric, it is best to go with a natural color and add dominant and bright colors for accenting. They are at their best in matte surfaces and traditional prints.

Hair

Classic people like their hair medium length. They don't like the fuss of looking after it, they like an easy style and length to manage. Classic style is desirable with no dramatic flare in coloring.

The Feminine Style

Mastering the feminine look requires elements that are draped and softly structured, in a modest length with small details and soft, textured fabrics. Feminine women love their natural fiber with matte-sheen in light to medium colors and prints.

Hair

Feminine people like their hair medium to long. They like the bounce and curls in their hair, because it gives them the feminine, natural look and feel that they desire. This look is light to medium in hair coloring and often adorned with hair accessories.

Bargain Business Suit

When bargain shopping for business attire, follow these steps. It's important to know the basic foundation for any business wardrobe is the suit. You will need black, navy, and lighter-colored suits (select camel or a pale gray for summer). For women with limited funds, wear your blazer with your skirts too. No need to buy a skirt suit. For shoes, keep the same in mind. Find at least three comfortable pairs of shoes, perhaps a pair of flats and two pairs of heels, one lower and the other a higher pump style.

I don't believe you should have all the colors of the rainbow on your shoe rack, especially when on a budget. Black and brown always work. Throw in a pair of camel or red for fun. The overall idea here is to have a bargain business wardrobe, classic pieces that won't go out of style and will last for years. Bargain notice, be on the lookout for sales and clearances. Wander through thrift stores. Be selective though. Buy quality bargain pieces and have them taken in by a seamstress if they aren't a perfect fit versus buying cheaper items.

Bargain Shoes that Last

Always buy quality shoes that last. Ensure that they are simple in color and style, are made of leather, and have a good sole and heel lifts. Shoes aren't made the way they used to be. Some shoes are plastic versus high quality rubber or leather. They wear down quickly, causing potential accidents. The shoe repair shop will replace and polish your shoes as needed, keeping the heels of your shoes looking new. In addition, shine your shoes regularly and buy scuff removing solution. A great pair of shoes can look like trash when they have not been taken care of.

Mastering the High Heels

I will admit I'm a lover of all shoe types. Wearing high heels came so naturally for me playing as a young child in my mother's high heels, running from closet to mirror, acting like I was in a fashion show. Practicing how to walk in high heels was something I looked forward to. Buying and wearing shoes is one of my weaknesses. For some of us, we look tall, sexy, sophisticated, and fabulous. For those who do not wear high heels but would like to, it will take a bit of practice. Start small and end tall. High heels make you feel fabulous and let you "strut your stuff" effortlessly! There are many heels to choose from, varying in height, thickness, and shape. It's important to train your feet and allow your ankles to develop the strength they need to walk safely, stylishly, and gracefully in high heels.

Carefully Choose Your Shoes

Not all high-heeled shoes are created the same. If you see an attractive pair of heels, try them on. Walk in them for a few moments. Are they comfortable? Do they rub up against your small toe, big toe, or heel? Here is a test of strength: Stand in your shoes on a hard floor with your knees straight. Check to see if you are able to raise yourself on your toes an inch. If you cannot do so, then the heels are too high for you right now and you shouldn't wear them. That does not mean you will never be able to wear them. So have confidence if you aim to wear tall heels one day.

Walking: The Art Form

Walking in heels is very different from walking in shoes. If you are new to the world of heels, be patient with yourself and allow yourself to "feel the heel." Walk with abbreviated steps and walk with confidence. Take small, slow steps and making sure you do not bend your knees any more than you normally would. Practice walking up and down stairs. Stairs can be tricky, so breathe and allow one foot to ascend or descend as you walk up or down stairs. Place one foot in front of the other and soon you will conquer your stairs. Take your time riding an escalator. Escalator rides can be tricky even in sneakers!

Practice, Practice, Practice

When you purchase that first pair of heels and you are assured of a great fit, practice wearing the heels at home first before you hit the public. Walk around the house in your heels and look at yourself in the mirror. How is your posture? How are your legs positioned? Try walking away from your mirror backwards as well as forwards. Change direction, stop, turn around, and pivot. Do all of the things you normally do in flat shoes.

Add Cushion When and Where Needed

Check your local drug store for great cushions. Do you need padding in the heel area or on your baby toe? Try your shoes on and allow your feet to "talk to you." Take a break. We want your feet to stay beautiful and bunion free, so take a break from wearing heels every day! Try opting for a great fall flat shoe in addition to your heels. Allow your shoes to take a break from the height. Your feet and toes will certainly thank you for it.

A Well-Rounded Woman

Communication

Always use politeness and be courteous to everyone (at least to their faces). It's counter productive to be combative and noncooperative. Try not to become excessively animated. People surround people who present a calm demeanor and a smooth, confident communication style.

Punctuality

This encompasses not only being on time, etc., but also organization. Nothing is more unprofessional than a person who is extremely messy, always late, or constantly absent.

Relationships

Professionals associate themselves with the top performers at the company. The people you surround yourself with reflect, the type of person you are. Also, forge a bond with your supervisors and bosses. They are your best allies in the company, so make sure to develop these relationships.

Appropriateness

As a boss, I've shared this insight with my team over and over. A lot of professional life is dictated by appropriateness. By "doing the right thing," even if that means "hurting" yourself in the short term, you are establishing an honest, hardworking, rock-solid reputation. Reputation is everything.

Right Signals

What should you do? This is one of those challenges that are completely within your control. Since you are the one who makes those purchases, you can practice "impression management." Simply put, you have the ability to dress so that the impressions others form about you are the impressions you want them to form. This is not to say there is no room for expressing your individuality, or that you have to buy expensive clothing—you must be able to communicate it in a way that also demonstrates your professional creativity, leadership potential, and confidence in yourself and your abilities.

Noticed

Notice what people you respect are wearing and start adjusting your wardrobe, building slowly. The importance of sending the correct messages cannot be stressed enough. Your professional image is the most important factor in showing management where you want to go within the organization. It can also help you gain the respect of colleagues, and establish instant trust and credibility with clients who are making critical decisions about your company and its products and services.

- *To make sure that your image communicates a high level of professionalism, I suggests making three words **Think**, **Reason**, and **Know**, your mantra when choosing your clothing or while shopping.*

- *Make sure your clothing consistently and appropriately complements your work environment.*

- *Demonstrate respect for yourself and others by considering how others view your clothing choices.*

You should always address the following three words prior to shopping: Think, Reason, and Know.

- ***Think** "wardrobe as investments." What is incorrect about your current wardrobe. What do you need to add?*

- *What is your primary **Reason** for "shopping." This is how I determine how to shop and build a fabulous wardrobe. I recommend that you be image and wardrobe conscious, using the essential pieces in your closet as your foundation. These are pieces you can call your sweet fabulous style.*

- *Before you head out, you need to **Know** the best "clothing choices for your body type." Start with the basics and add more as you can.*

Follow these three words when you plan to shop. It's an easy-to-use method that works.

More Must-Have Styles

If you are in doubt whether you can wear a piece of clothing with very strong colors, here you can find inspiration with fresh colors that will make you look like a perfect businesswoman. Here we present you with some creative ideas on how to make fabulous business combinations. Classic trousers and jackets are basic features of the modern businesswoman. They can give you classic glamour and elegance in movement in your outfit.

Know Your Style

Whether you have a job you want to keep or are searching for a new career, it is important to have the right items to demonstrate your professionalism. Women, we need to look at key pieces in our work wardrobe as investments. Always keep the most professional essential pieces in your closet. Be conscious about what you're wearing when important meetings pop up at the last minute. These are pieces you can incorporate in with your sweet, fabulous style, and they will work with each other.

- *Closed-toed black pumps, this is probably the most important investment in a professional woman's wardrobe.*

- *A simple black cardigan or a neutral color wrap sweater that can easily be paired with trousers, skirt, and over dresses creates a fabulous look on days you need to keep warm. A well-tailored white button-down blouse is the most classic top for pairing with separates. It can be worn under blazers, cardigans, wraps, and vests.*

- *The perfect cut skirt for your body type. Generally, if you have a narrow figure, meaning your hips are less defined, a low-cut, narrow skirt will work best for you, but you also have the ability to play with ruffles and other cuts without looking bulky. If you are a triangle shape, meaning your shoulders are the broadest part of your body, a skirt that falls straight and has a flare will compliment you most. For those with curves, pencil skirts were made just for you! A-line skirts work well for those with wider hips as well.*

- *Basic, classically cut trousers that are tailored to fit you. Make sure your pants aren't too snug on your rear, and that they fall straight and don't flare out. This is the most classic and flattering fit.*

- *Adaptable suit jacket/blazer that is clean and well-tailored. Choose something that is not too heavy and not too light. You want a jacket that will work with you year round.*

- *A dress that can easily transition from day to evening. Think sophisticated wrap dresses or sleek sweater dresses (utilizing the same rules as the best skirt for your body type).*

- *A professional handbag, one that has a closure. A handbag that is open, which is just a tote bag, looks messy and unpolished.*

- *Take a break from (boring) black tights, just for the trend's sake. To keep us all contemporary and not too classic (let's face it, too classic can definitely read as "boring" and who wants to look boring all the time?), it's fun to add a bit of fabulous personality to your look with some interesting tights. Tights are a professional wardrobe staple anyway, so why not swap out those plain black or nude nylons for a lace or floral pair that will add a bit of fabulous twist, yet sophisticated style to complete the look? You can also play with different colors and a plethora of other textures and designs that are available today. Have a fabulous time with it!*

- *Don't limit yourself to "classic" colors like black. While it's a safe bet, having a few pieces that add some color will help you create a more feminine, unique, and fabulous style.*

- *Think about something as simple as a skinny pink belt or dusty rose-colored shell. Just a small pop of color will lighten your entire look while keeping you fashion forward and professionally suited. Follow the steps in your personal guide notes as it will help you understand how to create a variety of looks and allow you to swap in accompanying tops, accessories, and other items for a long time to come, without you constantly needing to update your wardrobe. Have a fabulous time!*

Your Personal Study Guide Notes:

_____

_____

_____

_____

_____

_____

_____

_____

_____

_____

_____

_____

_____

_____

_____

_____

_____

_____

_____

_____

_____

_____

_____

8

Wardrobe

Dressing Style and Essentials

Your appearance at work should match your ambitions. An organized approach recommends visualizing the image you want to have once you've achieved your career goals. Do you look credible? Could you walk in the door tomorrow, take on that promotion and look the part? If not, you must build your current wardrobe. Remember, build your wardrobe for the job you want, not the one you have.

You just need to know the basics. Here are the essential items to add to your closet and how to wear them. Follow this guide book and you'll assemble an elegant, easy-to-use wardrobe that'll take you to the top of your game.

Women's Wardrobe Must Haves

- *Business wardrobe*
- *Conservative wardrobe*
- *Casual wardrobe*
- *Formal wardrobe*

A basic wardrobe includes a basic coat, suit with skirt and pants, several coordinated jackets, tops, blouses or sweaters, basic dress or jumper, basic outfit that could be worn for dress up or formal costume, basic rain coat, and sportswear.

Do you know how to create a fashion look all your own? How is your knowledge of color and your knowledge of fit? Can you set a clothing budget and make it work? Do you have a large selection of fashionable clothing in every style? Buy the best you can afford because the better-made clothes tolerate a lot of wear and tear. Buy clothes that are simple and look good for many different occasions.

Plan and Purchase

For this process of revamping your wardrobe, start noticing people you admire in your industry, your workplace and your position. Become keenly aware of the nuances of respected professionals in your field and you will usually pinpoint the right image. If you work in a more creative field, the looser, more relaxed style of "business casual" is acceptable. If you are in a corporate position or sales where you regularly meet with clients, opt for a formal, conservative look.

What to Wear to a Party

The bottom line. "If you want the job, you have to look the part," if you want the promotion, you have to look promotable. If you want respect, you have to dress at or above your industry standards. Prove that you're the life of any party with bold colors and prints. Choose a fabulous color with bags or shoes. If your outfit is very sophisticated, have your hair natural with loose curls. For attitude, listen to some girly fun songs before you go out that make you think you are confident and you don't care what the world thinks. With makeup, I'd say play up the eyes with a smoky look, but like brown and gold rather than black. Have fun, look polished and fabulous!

- *Pretty dress for parties and dates. It should be simple without a lot of trim and design details so you can wear different accessories with it to change the look.*

- *Clothes for your special lifestyle needs: Pants for bicycling, playing ball, yoga, zumba, running, swimming, etc.*

- *Warm coat for cold weather. Choose one large enough to wear over sweaters and other bulky clothes. It's best if you choose a neutral, solid color so you won't get tired of it and others won't remember it so well.*

- *Raincoat with zip-out lining. That way, you can take the lining out and wear it in dry but cold weather.*

- *Simple dresses look good with toss-on sweaters, jackets, or different scarves and belts.*

- *Purchase separates, blouses, sweaters, jackets, and skirts. Plan a wardrobe color scheme before you buy so you can coordinate all your separates and have an expensive look without spending a fortune.*

- *Also invest in a calf-leather briefcase after you've acquired a suit and shoes.*

- *Handbags that will go with everything. You can find those that have handles and a detachable shoulder strap. You need a small, plain handbag for dressy occasions.*

- *Shoes, two pairs of low-heels, two pairs of high-heels, pair of sneakers and boots.*

- *Stockings, socks, camisole, bras, panties, belts, scarves, watch, necklaces, earrings, and a fabulous quality piece of fine jewelry.*

Look Slimmer and Sexier

The Sexy Style

Part of the sexy style are dresses and skirts that are tight, body hugging, and show a trendy hemline. Any length is fine, short or long. The sexy style can be both in bold and daring or basic colors. The fabrics worn often have glitter and shine in them. Many are in animal prints with low-cut tops. The sexy women styles are glamorous, seductive, and feminine. Sexy people can be very curvy or slender in body form. The look gives one message and the message is exciting and compelling to the dress form. It's sexy and provocative.

Hair

Sexy women's hair, traditionally medium to long in length. Often it is styled to look uncontrolled and wild with curls, fullness and bounce. This style is worn in any solid color or may have some highlights around the face.

Sporty women love wearing their hair in a natural style, which is easy to care for at any length. They love to feel the movement of the hair and that's why they don't like the control of hairspray. They like to have their hair layered and free.

For classic women's hair, timeless styles are for them. They like their hair to be too controlled and neat. The idea is more in hair that is superbly cared for in an elegant style like a low bun in the back. No dramatic colors at all. They love the natural look. Classic women like their hair medium in length. They don't like the fuss of looking after it. They like an easy style and length to manage. Classic style is desirable with no dramatic flare in coloring.

Dramatic women's hair, usually kept in dramatic styles, strict and firm. She likes the look of slicking it back. Most dramatic women prefer dark-colored hair but like to add bold streaks and highlights to it. The preference is toward the extreme in length, which is either too long or too short for most other styles.

Related Links

- *The Most Wearable Fashion Trends for Spring*
- *12 Pretty Tights You Can Wear as Spring Looms*
- *Hair Accessories You Need to Make Life Easier*
- *Celebrities Sound Off on What Fame is Really Like*
- *Beauty Secrets of the Super Cool*
- *This Is What Badass Looks Like*
- *5 New Haircuts to Try This Season*
- *8 Phrases That Get His Attention Every Time*
- *The Best New Nude Polishes*
- *10 Celebrates with Swoon-Worthy Long Bobs*
- *18 Must-Have Espadrilles for Spring*

Your Personal Study Guide Notes:

_____

_____

_____

_____

_____

_____

_____

_____

_____

_____

_____

_____

_____

_____

_____

_____

_____

_____

_____

_____

_____

_____

9

Attitude

How ATTITUDES FORM, change and shape our behavior is the determining factor of whether our failure makes or breaks us. The persistence of a person who encounters failure is one sign of a healthy attitude. Winners don't quit! The guide book will teach you how to develop the attitude that brings that peace, success and confidence.

What Is an Attitude?

Psychologists define attitude as a learned tendency to evaluate things in a certain way. This can include evaluations of people, issues, objects, or events. Such evaluations are often positive or negative, but they can also be uncertain at times. For example, you might have mixed feelings about a particular person or issue.

Attitude can also be explicit and implicit. Explicit attitudes are those that we are consciously aware of and clearly influence our behaviors and beliefs. Implicit attitudes are unconscious, but still have an effect on our beliefs and behaviors.

Researchers also suggest there are several different components that make up attitudes.

1. *An Emotional Component: How the object, person, issue, or event makes you feel.*

2. *A Cognitive Component: Your thoughts and beliefs about the subject.*

3. *A Behavioral Component: How the attitude influences your behavior.*

How Do Attitudes Form?

Attitudes form directly as a result of experience. They may emerge due to direct personal experience or they may result from observation. Social roles and social norms can have a strong influence on attitudes. Social roles relate to how people are expected to behave in a particular role or context. Social norms involve society's rules for what behaviors are considered appropriate.

How Do Attitudes Influence Behavior?

We tend to assume people behave in accordance with their attitudes. However, social psychologists have found that attitudes and actual behavior are not always perfectly aligned. After all, plenty of people support a particular candidate or political party and yet fail to go out and vote.

Researchers have discovered people are more likely to behave according to their attitudes under certain conditions.

- *When your attitudes are the result of personal experience.*
- *When you are an expert in the subject.*

- *When you expect a favorable outcome.*

- *When the attitudes are repeatedly expressed.*

- *When you stand to win or lose something due to the issue.*

Attitude Change

While attitudes can have a powerful effect on behavior, they are not set in stone. The same influences that lead to attitude formation can also create attitude change.

- *Learning Theory of Attitude Change: Classical conditioning, operant conditioning, and observational learning, can be used to bring about attitude change. Classical conditioning can be used to create positive emotional reactions to an object, person, or event by associating positive feelings with the target object. Operant conditioning can be used to strengthen desirable attitudes and weaken undesirable ones. People can also change their attitudes after observing the behavior of others.*

- *Elaboration Likelihood Theory of Attitude Change: This theory of persuasion suggests that people can alter their attitudes in two ways. First, they can be motivated to listen and think about the message, thus leading to an attitude shift. Or they might be influenced by characteristics of the speaker, leading to a temporary or surface shift in attitude. Messages that are thought provoking and appeal to logic are more likely to lead to permanent changes in attitudes.*

- *Dissonance Theory of Attitude Change: As mentioned earlier, people can also change their attitudes when they have conflicting beliefs about a topic. In order to reduce the tension created by these incompatible beliefs, people often shift their attitudes.*

Finally, people also learn attitudes by observing the people around them. When someone you admire greatly espouses a particular attitude, you are more likely to develop the same beliefs. For example, children spend a great deal of time observing the attitudes of their parents and usually begin to demonstrate similar outlooks. The way we do in some cases, people may actually alter their attitudes in order to better align them with their behavior. Cognitive dissonance is a phenomenon in which a person experiences psychological distress due to conflicting thoughts or beliefs. In order to reduce this tension, people may change their attitudes to reflect their other beliefs or actual behaviors.

Imagine the following situation. You've always placed a high value on financial security, but you start dating someone who is very financially unstable. In order to reduce the tension caused by the conflicting beliefs and behavior, you have two options. You can end the relationship and seek out a partner who is more financially secure or you can de-emphasize the importance of fiscal stability. In order to minimize the dissonance between your conflicting attitude and behavior, you either have to change the attitude or change your actions.

Anger Management: 10 tips to tame your Temper

Are you ready to get your anger under control?

Keeping your temper in check can be challenging. Use simple anger management tips, from taking a timeout to using "I" statements to stay in control. Do you find yourself fuming when someone cuts you off in traffic? Does your blood pressure go through the roof when your child refuses to cooperate? Anger is a normal and even healthy emotion, but it's important to deal with it in a positive way. Uncontrolled anger can take a toll on both your health and your relationships.

Start by considering these 10 anger management tips

- **Take a timeout:** *Counting to ten isn't just for kids. Before reacting to a tense situation, take a few moments to breathe deeply and count to ten. Slowing down can help defuse your temper. If necessary, take a break from the person or situation until your frustration subsides a bit.*

- **Once you're calm, express your anger:** *As soon as you're thinking clearly, express your frustration in an assertive but non-confrontational way. State your concerns and needs clearly and directly, without hurting others or trying to control them.*

- **Get some exercise:** *Physical activity can provide an outlet for your emotions, especially if you're about to erupt. If you feel your anger escalating, go for a brisk walk or run, or spend some time doing other favorite physical activities. Physical activity stimulates various brain chemicals that can leave you feeling happier and more relaxed than you were before you worked out.*

- **Think before you speak:** *In the heat of the moment, it's easy to say something you'll later regret. Take a few moments to collect your thoughts before saying anything—and allow others involved in the situation to do the same.*

- **Identify possible solutions:** *Instead of focusing on what made you mad, work on resolving the issue at hand. Does your child's messy room drive you crazy? Close the door. Is your partner late for dinner every night? Schedule meals later in the evening or agree to eat on your own a few times a week. Remind yourself that anger won't fix anything and might only make it worse.*

- **Anger issues in women:** *Anger issues in women are becoming increasingly common. Here's how to manage your anger.*

When men get angry, nobody bats an eyelid, but when a woman's temper gets the better of her, it becomes headline news. The spate of recent reports on schoolyard violence among girls has dominated current affairs programs over the past few months, yet when boys fight in the playground, it's somehow deemed normal.

- *Violence in women: This is becoming more prevalent than ever. The amount of women prosecuted for domestic violence has risen by 11 percent in the past ten years. The number of women arrested for violent crimes is 40 percent higher than in 2005 and female road rage is more common than ever. So why have women started to get angry? It may be as simple as the fact that females have increasing amounts of pressure and responsibility piled on them today.*

- *Are we doing too much: "Many women today are over-extended," explains Melbourne-based anger management expert Meghan Birks. "Women are under a lot of pressure to do it all, work full-time, look after the family and still look good. When we're so busy, it doesn't allow time to be still and check in with you, which can be a big cause of pent-up anger and frustration." Many women try and hold in their anger, which in the long term can only make things worse. Birks says, "It's not seen as feminine to get angry. It's much more acceptable for men to lose their temper." But holding your frustrations in can mean your anger build up and is let out at inappropriate moments. Birks warns, "Many people get angry over small things, such as someone cutting in on them on the road. Although it may appear that this is what has triggered an angry outburst, it's likely they're actually upset about something that has happened previously which they haven't been able to express." Some experts believe seeing violence on TV could also be contributing to the problem. On US TV, violence against women has increased by 120 percent in the past five years. "Seeing violence and anger around us all the time sends the message that it's a normal way of express-*

ing yourself," Birks says. "But there are much more effective ways to communicate that you're upset, like talking rationally about your feelings." It's also important to realize that even if you aren't outwardly shouting and screaming, you could still be experiencing anger.

- **Expressing Anger:** "Depression is sometimes described as 'anger turned inwards,'" Birks says. "When women don't know how to deal with their emotions, they may internalize their anger. Keeping all these feelings inside can lead to depression." Not only does anger suppress your immune system, it can also destroy relationships. "People end up tiptoeing around you because they become nervous about when you're going to fly off the handle," Birks says. Taking your anger out on children can be particularly detrimental. "Children don't understand it's not them who made you angry. All they see is someone shouting at them. They can absorb those emotions and start to think that's the correct way to react if someone is upset. Of course, sometimes it's perfectly acceptable to be angry," says Dr. Vesna Grubacevic, a clinical hypnotherapist who specializes in anger issues. "There are some situations where you are perfectly within your rights to feel angry," she says. "If someone has deliberately hurt or betrayed you, then of course you're allowed to feel angry and upset." The important thing is to differentiate between unresolved and resolved anger. Resolved anger means reacting proportionately in an appropriate way to a situation. Unresolved anger, such as road rage, is when you fly off the handle at a situation that doesn't warrant it. If you're constantly showing signs of unresolved anger, you need to think seriously about whether your temper is getting out of control. "If people appear shocked by how you're acting, chances are you've got an issue you need to deal with," Dr. Grubacevic advises.

- **Getting Help:** Talking to an anger management expert can help you deal with anger issues, but there are plenty of other things you can do to improve the situation. "The way you treat *your body affects your anger levels," Birks explains. "Eating lots of additives and sugar can make you agitated and angry. Not exercising enough can also be a factor." Then you need to take an honest look at your life and think about your priorities. "You don't have to do everything that's thrown at you," Birks says. "Saying 'no' allows you to take control of the situation. Many people say they're angry because they feel they have no control over their lives. Take that control back and you'll feel calmer."*

When you feel yourself getting angry, take a physical step backward before reacting, I tell my children, "Take a deep breath and count to ten. It sounds clichéd, but it really does reduce the heat from the situation and allows you to think before you act."

Finally, it's important to realize that anger is often futile. "If someone cuts in on you in the car and you spend the next hour feeling angry about it, the only person you're damaging is yourself. Think of anger as throwing a hot coal at someone; you'll blister your own fingers, but the person you throw the rock at will probably walk away unscathed."

Remember, use the meditation technique above to reduce short-term anger, as advised by Dr. Vesna Grubacevic.

Things Women Need to Know

- *How to stay calm: Pick a spot in front of you above eye level, such as the top of your computer screen. Focus intently on that spot, keeping your head still. Then, without moving your head, start to notice everything in your peripheral vision, such as furniture and people. Focus on that spot for two minutes. You'll start to feel calmer and more connected with everyone around you.*

- *Vent through expressing your anger: This can be good for you. Flying into a rage at every suspected slight isn't the answer. For instance, blowing off steam by hurling hardware at your hubby or breaking plates over the boss's head aren't great solutions. But it is possible, even desirable, to use anger in a positive rather than negative way.*

- ***Forget the pop notion of channeling anger into more productive pursuits:*** *"Relationship enhancement is the most productive outlet possible for anger," says Deborah Cox, PhD, a psychologist at Southwest Missouri State University in Springfield and this can happen when you let the other person see you're upset. So, what concrete tips might help when you're mad as hell and not going to take it anymore? Read on.*

- ***Martha Stewart Comes Clean:*** *By Jenny Allen the domestic diva opens up about the pain in her past, the love in her life, and how she bounced back big time. Martha Stewart takes a forkful of lemon pie and savors it. "Isn't this good?" she asks in that trademark low, plumy voice. We're lunching in her office at the Manhattan TV studio where she's just finished hosting a live broadcast of The Martha Stewart Show, her Emmy award-winning daily program. She sits at one end of the sleek rectangular table that...*

  http://connection.ebscohost.com/c/articles/27047795/ martha-comes-clean.

- *Seek out a safe place to see. Before confronting the object of your wrath, talk with a trusted friend, co-worker, or counselor who can help get to the root of what's pressing your buttons. Mulling it over with someone safe may help you figure out less hostile, more instructive ways to express your feelings with a loved one, colleague, or boss.*

- *Approach the person who sent your blood boiling in the first place. As a general guideline, the more significant the relationship, the more important it is to articulate feelings in a constructive way, says Dana Crowley Jack, EdD, a psychologist at Fairhaven College at Western Washington University* in Bellingham. She suggests trying something like, *This is bothering me. Something has to change. How can we deal with it?"*

- *Identify the reason behind the rage.* There's always something underlying an angry reaction. The trick here is to find the trigger. If it is not obvious, keeping a log of anger experiences may help you uncover patterns. For some people, professional help may be needed to delve through deep-rooted feelings of shame and anger that started in childhood.

- *Find a physical release.* Though jogging and other physical activities can be helpful, Cox advocates an anger workout: Hitting a mattress with a tennis racket or slapping the sofa with a bat when you really start to see red. The key, says Cox, is to talk as you whack the furniture. Engaging large muscle groups along with your voice should help you work through some of your fury. Kickboxing or Tae-Bo may give the same results. You'll feel less likely to lose it if you have a physical release first, explains Cox. "When a client tells me: 'If I really let it out, we'd all burst into flames,' then I might suggest an anger workout," she says.

- *Take several deep breaths.* If you find yourself blinded by heat-of-the-moment anger, try to buy some time to cool off a bit, especially if you think you're at risk of harming someone physically or emotionally. You may even need to walk away from the situation for a while. Remember, though, that in the long run, fleeing the scene won't help you express yourself. So ask for a few moments to collect your thoughts and then say what needs to be said.

- *Look for like-minded souls.* All fired up about a societal injustice? Sick of suffering? Then hook up with people who share your passion or problem through a support group or organization. Consider working with an organization for change, like Mothers against Drunk Driving (MADD). "Joining other *people who care about what you do can transform anger into a positive expression," says Jack.*

Anger is a painful state of mind. When you develop anger, you lose your inner peace of mind and your body becomes uncomfortable and tense. In an angry state, it is impossible to fall a sleep or even enjoy food. The common shortcoming of anger is the failure to reason and even losing one's good sense. When people are in an anger state, they tend to risk their life looking for a way to take revenge on those who have harmed them. In fact, a number of deaths and serious injuries have resulted due to lack of anger management. The other unfortunate character of anger is that it is a blind rage. When you are in anger state, you forget about the good things done to you by the person. This unfortunate behavior can often lead to isolation as close friends and family stay away to protect themselves.

Therefore, if you are a person who is unable to control anger, it is necessary to seek help before it is too late. If you can catch and admit to this bad behavior at an early stage, you do not have to reschedule your lifestyle as you can learn different ways on managing your anger at home through online courses. However, when selecting the ideal course, it is necessary to understand that women display anger differently from men. While male anger is associated with aggression and aggressive behavior, the major aspects of female anger include feelings of powerlessness, violations of basic values, and lack of reciprocity in intimate relationships. They are most often not displayed with any physically aggressive behavior.

In order to manage and understand your anger, you need to look at the specific challenges and create methods that work for your situation. Nevertheless, you can use various anger management techniques for women to manage and resolve your anger problems. The first step is to understand your anger. This includes situations, feelings, motivations, and actions that trigger your anger.

The second step is to analyze your anger tendencies. You need to understand the effect of anger on you. The majority of women tend to repress their anger, which is unhealthy. Repressing anger for long might cause certain health effects such as frequent headaches, irritable bowel syndrome or stomach aches, among other serious conditions.

The third step in anger management techniques for women is analyzing the anger pattern. In this stage, look at issues such as how you behave when angry. Do you cry, become abusive, or retract into yourself? Also understand whether you express anger to certain people and hide it on others.

The fourth step is to recognize your anger trigger. You should take enough time to come up with the common triggers of your anger. It is necessary to note that everyone has certain issues that trigger anger.

The fifth step in anger management techniques for women is to learn about your behaviors and beliefs. A large number of women create anger for themselves by dwelling much on past injuries or hurts. The other self-inflicting trigger is unrealistic expectation of others. If your anger is triggered by unrealistic expectations, you need to adjust your demands, otherwise, no training will help.

The sixth factor that you need to consider is from whom you learned to express your anger. You might have learned poor anger management through an association with another person. Understanding these steps will help you come up with a feasible anger management solution.

Online anger management courses provide the most current techniques, skill, and education on how to deal with anger. They are affordable and can be taken in the privacy of your own home. They are available from the AJ Novick Group and there is a licensed therapist available to speak with Monday through Friday if you have any questions or concerns while reviewing the course. Learning the tools you need to successfully combat your anger control issue is the best gift you can give yourself.

Your Personal Study Guide Notes:

_____

_____

_____

_____

_____

_____

_____

_____

_____

_____

_____

_____

_____

_____

_____

_____

_____

_____

_____

_____

_____

_____

_____

_____

_____

_____

10

Career Guide

THE CAREER GUIDE and job search listed below are designed to assist you in the career planning and job search process. Select the desired topics and enter them in your favorite search engine for more information.

Career Exploration and Experience

- *General Employment Strategies*
- *Building Linked In Presence*
- *Creating Career Objective*
- *Dressing to Impress*
- *Negotiating Job Offers*
- *Preparing for a Telephone Interview*

- *Preparing for the First Interview*
- *Preparing for your Second Interview*
- *Researching Potential Employers*
- *Using Internet in Your Job Search*
- *Using Proper Etiquette*
- *Writing Effective Letters*
- *Writing a Resume*
- *Preparing for Career Fair*

Targeted Employment Strategies

- *Finding a Summer Job*
- *Interviewing for a Faculty Position*
- *Searching for a Job in Human Services*
- *Searching for a Job as Student*
- *Searching for an International Job*
- *Searching for a Part-time Job*
- *Searching for a Temporary Job*
- *Starting Your Small Business*
- *Transitioning from the Military*
- *Working Abroad*

User's Guides for Career Center Tools

- *Career Portfolio User's Guide*
- *Using Career Portfolio in an Academic Job Search*
- *Seminole Link User's Guide*

Creating Four Academic and Career Plans

- *Choosing a Major*
- *Choosing a Major: A Guide for Families*
- *Conducting Information Interviews*
- *Finding and using Graduate Student Resources*
- *Going to Graduate School*
- *Making the Most of Your Internship*
- *Co-op Work Experience*
- *Preparing for Internships and Co-ops*
- *Preparing Portfolio*
- *Preparing Resume*
- *Studying Abroad*
- *Writing Personal Statements*

Using Social Media

- *Facebook*
- *Create a New Job Alert*
- *Post Your Resume on Job Links*
- *Linked In*
- *The Boss Group*

10 Richest Countries in the World

▲	Country	GDP
1.	United States	$15,940,000,000,000
2.	China	$12,610,000,000,000
3.	India	$4,761,000,000,000
4.	Japan	$4,704,000,000,000
5.	Germany	$3,250,000,000,000
6.	Russia	$2,555,000,000,000
7.	Brazil	$2,394,000,000,000
8.	United Kingdom	$2,375,000,000,000
9.	France	$2,291,000,000,000
10.	Italy	$1,863,000,000,000

Did you know the richest?

- *Countries with Largest Economies*
- *Most Generous Countries*
- *World's Largest Humanitarian Donors*
- *Countries with Highest Income per Capital*
- *Richest Countries in the Middle East*

- *Richest Countries in Africa*
- *Richest Countries in Asia*
- *Richest Countries in South America*
- *Richest Countries in the Caribbean*
- *Richest Countries in Central America*
- *Countries with the Most Billionaires*
- *Countries with the Most Millionaires*
- *Countries with the Highest Density of Millionaires*
- *Richest People in the World*
- *Richest People in History*
- *Richest Women in the World*

Did you know the most?

- *Happiest Countries*
- *Most Educated Countries*
- *Dangerous Countries to Live In*
- *Least Happy Countries*
- *Countries with the Biggest TV Watchers*
- *Developing Countries*
- *Cheapest Countries to Travel To*
- *Best Cities*
- *Safest Countries for Children*
- *Countries with the Best Health Care*
- *Highest National Debt*
- *Countries with the Highest Employment Rates*
- *Countries with the Incidence of Breast Cancer*
- *Highest Illiteracy Rates*

- *Dangerous Cities*
- *Cleanest Cites*
- *Countries with the Largest Overweight Populations*
- *Worst Cities*
- *Highest Birth Rates*
- *Highest Paying Jobs*
- *Expensive Cities*
- *Most Populous States in America*
- *Most Polite Cities in the World*

Did you know the highest?

- *Countries with the Highest Quality of Life*
- *Countries with the Lowest Rate of Deaths from Road Accidents*
- *Most Dangerous Cities in America*
- *Highest Teenage Pregnancy Rates in Developed Countries*
- *Best Cities for Singles in America*
- *Most Depressing Jobs*
- *Most Generous Countries*
- *Poorest Countries in the World*
- *Richest Countries in the World*
- *Most Affordable US Cities*
- *Countries with Highest Suicide Rates*
- *Highest Polluted Cities*
- *Safest Cities in America*
- *Countries with the Highest Obesity Rates*

11

Women with Authority

Women in Power The Fifteen Highest Paid

BLOOMBERG RECENTLY RANKED the women who are named executive officers of S&P 500 companies based on their total compensation for the latest fiscal year. It's an interesting list below:

Women Executives

1. **Safra Catz**
   Title: Co-President/CFO
   Company: Oracle
   Industry: Software
   Pay, latest fiscal year: $51,700,000

2. **Marissa Mayer**
   Title: President/CEO
   Company: Yahoo!
   Industry: Media Content
   Pay, latest fiscal year: $36,620,000

3. **Irene Rosenfeld**
   Title: Chairman/CFO
   Company: Mondelez International
   Industry: Consumer Products
   Pay, latest fiscal year: $28,810,000

4. **Sharen Turney**
   Title: President/CEO, Victoria's Secret
   Company: Limited Brand Inc.
   Industry: Retail Discretionary
   Pay, latest fiscal year: $25,620,000

5. **Carol Meyrowitz**
   Title: CEO
   Company: TJX Companies
   Industry: Retail Discretionary
   Pay, latest fiscal year: $21,770,000

6. **Angela Braly**
   Title: Chairman/President/CEO
   Company: WellPoint
   Industry: Health Care Facilities/Services
   Pay, latest fiscal year: $20,590,000

7. **Virginia Rometty**
   Title: Chairman/President/CEO
   Company: IBM

Industry: Technology Services
Pay, latest fiscal year: $16,180,000

8. **Ellen Kullman**
   Title: Chairman/CEO
   Company: DuPont
   Industry: Chemicals
   Pay, latest fiscal year: $15,660,000

9. **Meg Whitman**
   Title: President/CEO
   Company: Hewlett-Packard
   Industry: Hardware
   Pay, latest fiscal year: $15,360,000

10. **Renee James**
    Title: Executive VP/General Manager, Software
    Company: Intel
    Industry: Semiconductors
    Pay, latest fiscal year: $15,300,000

11. **Mary Erdoes**
    Title: CEO, Asset Management
    Company: JPMorgan Chase
    Industry: Institutional Financial Service
    Pay, latest fiscal year: $14,750,000

12. **Rosalind Brewer**
    Title: President/CEO, Sam's Club
    Company: Wal-Mart Stores
    Industry: Retail Staples
    Pay, latest fiscal year: $14,460,00

13. Indra Nooyi
Chairman and CEO, PepsiCo, Inc.
Industry: Consumer Products
Compensation: $14,210,000

14. Ursula Burns
Chairman and CEO, Xerox
Industry: Hardware
Compensation: $13,070,000

15. Sheri McCoy
Chairman and CEO, Avon Products
Industry: Consumer Products
Compensation: $12,930,000

Methodology

Bloomberg ranked women who are named executive officers of S&P 500 companies based on their total compensation for the latest fiscal year. Figures were taken from companies' proxy statements. Included were executives who weren't in their posts for the full year: Angela Braly left WellPoint in August 2012 and both Marissa Mayer of Yahoo! and Sheri McCoy of Avon became CEOs during 2012. Renee James was named president of Intel in April 2013.

Best Jobs for Women

"Whether you're still in school and figuring out what career to pursue or on the hunt for something new, we rounded up the absolute best jobs for women out there," says Molly Triffin.

- *Physician: Health care jobs are booming, thanks to the aging population and there's a particular need for more general practitioners. Family doctors make a great salary ($177,000* *on average), sans the crazy shifts that many MDs work. Plus, since you get a ton of one-on-one interaction with patients, it's a good bet if you're a people person.*

- ***Market Research Analyst:*** *Like figuring out what makes people tick? Market research analysts help companies understand what products and services customers want, by organizing focus groups, parsing through sales data, and developing strategic plans. The salary's about $61,000 and with a 41 percent growth rate, an additional 117,000 new jobs will pop up by 2020.*

- ***Physician's Assistant:*** *Want to treat and diagnose patients, make bank ($86,000 annually), but avoid six years of med school and student loan debt? Consider becoming a physician's assistant. You'll do examinations, administer tests, make diagnoses, and recommend courses of treatment, think Dr. House, minus the bad attitude. This field is on the rise, with 30 percent growth this decade, so once you have your degree (it requires a master's), you'll be pretty set.*

- ***Video Game Designer:*** *Want to make every dude you meet worship the ground you walk on? If you're super creative and have some tech skills (like web design or coding), being the creator of Man-Eating Zombies III could be your calling. It's a lot of pressure, but you'll make about $81,000 to build games from scratch, come up with cool concepts and work closely in a team. Hint: Networking is crucial because it's competitive.*

- ***Health Care Technology Manager:*** *This career hits the sweet spot between two rapidly rising fields: Health care and IT. You'll manage patient records, create databases and make a cool eighty-three grand a year. Since it's still relatively uncommon, competition is slim but demand is huge. You'll need a bachelor's degree in computer programming, software development, or health care (with tech skills on the side).*

- *Physical Therapist:* This is another awesome option that's highly marketable, now that all those baby boomers want to fix their aches and pains. The pay's reasonable, about $76,000, and there's an expected 39 percent increase in growth by 2020, so chances are you'll be able to score a position. The hours are decent and it's personally rewarding, you'll watch the patients you're treating become stronger and healthier under your care.

- *Information Security Analyst:* If you're an adrenaline junkie and have tech smarts, check out this high-paying, in-demand career. You're on the frontlines of the fight against hackers, figuring out how to prevent networks from being broken into and corrupted, all for $76,000 per year.

- *Landscape Architect:* If you're an artsy nature lover, then designing parks, gardens, and other spaces could be your dream gig! As the real estate market rebounds and going green is bigger than ever, demand for landscape architects is expected to rise. To nab the $62,000-a-year job, it helps to get a specialized degree and internships or apprenticeships are must-haves.

- *Digital Strategist:* Play around online all day…and get paid about $60,000 for it? Yes, please! Digital strategists advise clients on how to improve their tech presence, making websites user-friendly and entertaining, etc. You don't need a specific degree to nab one of these jobs, but digital experience helps and you have to be on the cutting edge of the latest technology and social media trends like Facebook, Twitter, and Pinterest.

- *Reputation Manager:* It's the hot new PR job, think Scandal on a smaller scale. Fine-tune a company's online presence by strategically tweaking its website, social media platforms and search results to making sure it has a positive image for an average annual pay of $58,000.

- *ESL or GED Instructor:* If teaching appeals to you, but dealing with a classroom of noisy, snot-nosed rugrats sounds hell-

ish, consider adult education. For about $47,000 a year, you'll help people learn basic skills reading, writing, speaking English or coach them to earn their GED. Most instructors have a bachelor's degree and teaching certificate.

- *Interior Designer: With the housing market making a comeback, decorating is set to have a moment too. As long as you have a gift for it and you network like crazy, you don't need special schooling. You can even segue into it while keeping your day job: Offer to make over your first ten clients' homes for free (ask family and friends) and word of mouth will get your name around. Plan to make around $46,000 and since you're your own boss, you can avoid annoying office politics and get to set your own hours and vacations.*

- *Interpreter: With a 42 percent predicted increase in open positions, there's tons of opportunity. You'll work in hospitals, schools or courtrooms, translating info for those who don't speak the language. You need to be fluent in both English and a second language and the average salary is $43,000.*

- *Group Personal Trainer: Fitness instructors score serious perks: Flexible schedules, low stress, being able to live in yoga, and getting paid to work out (the average salary is just $31,000, but it's a growing market). According to the American College of Sports Medicine, small group personal training, outdoor personal training, Zumba, and core fitness will all be big in 2013.*

Related links

5 Easy Ways to Get a Raise at Work

Best Work-at-Home Jobs

Earn a steady paycheck without ever leaving your house

Best Top Home-Based Professions

If you don't relish the thought of hustling to a workplace every day or you're having a hard time securing a local gig, there's never been a better time to work from home: More than forty million Americans do it, according to the advocacy group Telework Coalition. And as the economy improves, more companies will be looking for additional staff. For most at-home jobs, you'll need a computer and an Internet connection, some basic skills, and a can-do attitude. Click through this list of seven employment areas that are booming right now. (Daisy Chan).

The Job: Direct Salesperson

What It Pays

It depends on the company, but you typically take home 20 to 35 percent of sales in commissions.

Perfect For

Someone with an entrepreneurial spirit, loads of energy and a love of meeting new people.

What It Is

Think Avon or Mary Kay, you organize get-togethers to sell a company's wares, whether those are bath products, gardening supplies, books, or wine. Over time, you build a base of clients.

How to Get It

You can apply directly through the companies, such as Stella & Dot, a jewelry company that had over $100 million in sales in 2010. A few other good ones include Silpada (jewelry), The Pampered Chef (kitchenware) and Dove Chocolate Discoveries. You can also visit the Direct Selling Association website at DirectSelling411.org, all the companies listed there agree to abide by a code of ethics, so they only offer legitimate opportunities. Typically reps make a small investment to get started (this is a legitimate and standard practice) and sometimes pay a fee for the merchandise being sold. After that you can work as much or as little as you want and see profit based on how much you sell.

The Job: Corporate English Trainer

What It Pays

Around $15 an hour

Perfect For

Native English speakers with basic computer skills and an interest in other cultures who love chatting online or over the phone. Office experience is very helpful, since most students work in a corporate environment. You also need your own computer and a high-speed Internet connection. If you're bilingual, that's a plus.

What It Is

Students in countries including Japan, Korea, France and Germany are looking for English speakers to practice with. Sessions focus on things like making professional small talk or running a meeting (trainers are provided with specifics on how to teach each topic and are also trained themselves for two days before starting the job). Lessons take place either over the phone or on a live Internet video service like Skype, sometimes at night, because you're working with students in different time zones. You need to commit to a minimum of twenty hours a week at consistent times and can work as many as thirty-five hours.

How to Get It

GoFluent.com is an English training company working with twelve of the world's largest corporations. There are also jobs out there for English as a Second Language (ESL) teachers, which are more structured. Visit ISUS (iSpeakUSpeak.com), a placement and training company. While a degree in education or ESL is ideal, you are encouraged to apply if you are enthusiastic and articulate.

The Job: Telephone Nurse

What It Pays

Competitive with a regular nursing salary, this is $50,000 or more

Perfect For

Someone with a Nursing Degree

What It Is

Health insurers or other health management companies, including Humana, Aetna and UnitedHealth Group, hire nurses remotely to perform duties like case management, treatment authorization and patient education.

How to Get It

To find the right position for you, check out the listings at major medical-job placement firms likeMedicalJobsOnline.com, The Judge Group (Judge.com) and MedZilla (Medzilla.com).

The Job: Search Engine Evaluator

What It Pays

$9 to $10 an hour

Perfect For

English speakers who are up on movies and music, as well as those familiar with other cultures.

What It Is

Companies like Google and Yahoo! give you information to search for and you tell them how closely their results matched what you were looking for. Does a search for Lady Antebellum turn up sites about the music group or links to pre–Civil War period information? If you are Latina, for example, you might be asked to search the way a Spanish speaker might perform a search in English. Jobs are usually between ten to twenty-five hours a week.

How to Get It

Most companies hire through firms like Leapforce At Home (LeapforceAtHome.com) and Appen Butler Hill (AppenButler-Hill.com).

The Job: Customer Service Representative

What It Pays

$8 to $18 an hour

Perfect For

"People" people with patience to spare who are good at talking on the phone while on the computer.

What It Is

Companies are looking for workers with excellent speaking abilities and solid computer skills to help customers find a correct size, place an order or resolve a conflict. Both full-and-part-time positions are available and you are generally required to devote a four-hour block of time.

How to Get It

Customer service is the biggest work-at-home field, with companies including Spiegel, Hilton, Best Western, HSN, 1-800-FLOW-ERS, and many others using at-home reps. Fill out an application with staffing companies such as Arise (Arise.com), Alpine Access (AlpineAccess.com), VIPdesk (VIPdesk.com), LiveOps (LiveOps.com), and Convergys (Convergys.com), all of which vet the companies who are hiring through them. If you need benefits, search through a staffing company that will hire you as an employee (Alpine Access, VIPdesk, and Convergys do this) rather than an independent contractor. If you're a contractor, you may be asked to pay a small fee (between $15 and $35) for a background check. While a fee can be a sign of a scam, independent contractors are responsible for their own expenses.

The Job: Online Teacher

What It Pays

The average salary for the first year is around $30,000; teachers of some subjects are paid more than others.

Perfect For

Teachers who don't want a typical school schedule.

What It Is

Instead of standing in a classroom, you'll teach via Skype or in a prerecorded session. There is a growing demand for teachers in all subjects, but especially core topics like English, history and science.

How to Get It

Check out K12 (K12.com) and Connections Academy (Connec-tionsAcademy.com). Both organizations offer various benefits, including health insurance, retirement savings accounts, and paid time off, depending on where you live. As in any job where you work with kids, there will be a background and reference check as well as interviews. You may also need to be licensed to teach in the state where the students reside.

The Job: Virtual Tutor

What It Pays

$12 to $35 an hour

Perfect For

People who only have pockets of time to work and an extensive knowledge of or expertise in a subject or are fluent in a foreign language.

What It Is

You work with a student who needs extra help, usually for a half hour over the phone or Skype.

How to Get It

Sylvan Learning (Tutoring.SylvanLearning.com), Tutor.com, Tu-torVista.com, and Tutorzilla (Tutorzilla.com) all offer a good cross section of the kinds of remote-based tutoring jobs out there and they all have great reputations with students and teachers. Since you will be working with children, you can expect a background check before you are hired.

Sources: Christine Durst, cofounder, RatRaceRebellion.com. Holly Hanna, founder of TheWorkAtHomeWoman.com blog,

Amy Robinson, chief marketing officer, Direct Selling Association.
Lois Greisman, associate director, division of marketing, FTC.

Related Links

1. *10 Smart Ways to Make Money from Home*
2. *8 New Ways to Work from Home*
3. *3 Sites for Working from Home*
4. *How to Make Money at Home*
5. *WD on TV Make Money Online*
6. *5 Best Online Deals Home Linens*
7. *Top 10 Work-at-Home Scams*
8. *3 Stylish Work-from-Home Looks*
9. *10 Ways to Make Money from Home*

Your Personal Study Guide Notes:

_____

_____

_____

_____

_____

_____

_____

_____

_____

_____

_____

_____

_____

_____

_____

_____

_____

_____

_____

_____

_____

_____

_____

_____

12

Fabulous and Successful Women

President, CEO, Philanthropist, and Executive

I BELIEVE IN focusing on a positive future outcome. I am dedicated to bringing positive change to the face of health, fashion, media, and recognized brands. A movement. A Change for Lives!

Lauren Freeman

Founder and CEO of Lauren Fabulous Firm, LLC an organization dedicated to improving women's lifestyles, building a strong platform that helps women lead better lives, a firm that promotes Fabulous Women leaders, their images, beauty, careers, and lifestyles globally.

What advice would you give women who are considering a new career?

Don't wait on the next new trend, *be* the next new trend. Know who you are… and who you should be. Find your gift and understand what it takes to master your gift. Have a clear vision of where you are and where you want to go. Know your flawless role, based on your personal experiences, education, and career goals. Do what you love, own it and do you!

I enjoy giving advice on how to overcome obstacles, the value of getting established, undertaking responsibilities, we're an organization dedicated to bringing positive change.

Anne Lynam Goddard

President and CEO of Child Fund International, a global child development organization dedicated to helping children in poverty thrive and bring positive change to their communities.

What advice would you give women who are considering a new career?

Learn as much as you can about your chosen field from every perspective. Take on jobs or responsibilities that you're not crazy about so you can learn. The better-rounded you are in your field, the more effective you will be at work, and the more attractive you will be to prospective employers. Also, as an employer and leader, I am most interested in the results people produce rather than whether they're working long hours.

What's the most important thing to remember when it comes to your personal life?

It's more important than your job! My relationships with my family are more valuable and long-lasting than any career. It's loving others and being loved in return that gives real purpose and satisfaction in life. Marry someone with the same values as you; it will make critical decisions that you need to make together so much easier.

How did you overcome your biggest career hurdle?

I once got a new boss whom I perceived had a not-so-positive impression of me that was hindering my career. So I asked him to be my mentor; he agreed and we met on a regular basis for three months. Through our discussions he got to know me much better and when a promotional opportunity came up, he was my biggest advocate and I got the job.

Suzi Weiss-Fischmann

Executive VP and artistic director of OPI nail products

What advice would you give to women who want to follow in your footsteps?

I think it's important to be focused. Of course, there will be many bumps along the way, but don't get distracted by the zigzags in the road. Vision and passion are very clear; if you believe in something, other people will too.

How do you think a woman can successfully balance her career and personal life?

My best advice is, don't forget about "me" time. Schedule a window of time for yourself, like any other appointment, if you have to. In the end, taking personal time will make you more productive at work.

What do you know now that you wish you had known when you were younger?

I wish I had known how important patience and listening can be. These are two qualities that are often overlooked, but can be very helpful in both your career and personal life.

Gayle Tzemach Lemmon

Deputy director of the Council on Foreign Relations Women and Foreign Policy program, and author of *The Dressmaker of Khair Khana*.

What's the key to a successful career?

Always remember that hard work is necessary to achieve your biggest dreams. Your social life will suffer at intervals, but remember your goals and know that this is part of the journey toward achieving your dreams. When I was finishing a Newsweek cover story about Secretary of State Hillary Clinton, I was nine months pregnant and often thought about napping rather than returning to my computer! But I focused on the mission and I kept working.

What got you through tough times at work?

I was finishing the first round of research for *The Dressmaker of Khair Khana* in the fall of 2008 and kept encountering setback after setback. Security in Afghanistan was awful and the families I interviewed often suggested I go home and return another time. But I knew this was the work I was there to do and that my job was to tell a story celebrating the unsung heroines all around us who never back down to fear. It was my responsibility to see the work through and to bring this book and this story to life about the young women who supported their communities during the Taliban control.

What's the biggest career mistake you've made?

Worrying. During my 20s I worried that every decision would have irrevocable consequences and that there was only one path. The truth is that there are many paths and what looks like a setback today may next year turn out to have been a blessing.

Lenise Bent

DreamWorks sound engineer and instructor at SAE Institute, Los Angeles, which provides education for careers in the recording and post-production industries.

How can someone achieve long-term success in his or her career?

If anyone, male or female, is passionate about a certain field, he or she will do whatever it takes to make it a career. If you are doing it to get thanks, you are doing it for the wrong reasons. Do something because you love it, not for recognition.

What gets you through tough times at work?

I tell myself, "I'm not a successful woman engineer; I'm a successful engineer who is also a woman." There's a big difference. Knowing what you are working toward and keeping in mind the big picture when things get tough or complicated is essential.

What do you know now that you wish you had known when you were younger?

When I was younger I dressed asexually and wore my glasses so the client and studio would know I was serious about becoming an engineer/producer. What I finally realized was that getting more experience was most important; I made myself an asset to the project by anticipating what was needed, taking initiative and being fun to be around. Once I established my reputation, I was good to go.

Sepi Asefnia

President of SEPI Engineering, a North Carolina–based civil engineering firm.

How did you overcome your biggest career hurdle?

Since I was born in Iran and was a woman entering a male-dominated industry, I encountered plenty of obstacles getting myself established in civil engineering. The lack of any family or peer connections in the field didn't help either. What did help was that I had confidence in my abilities and when I faced roadblocks, I employed two strategies. The first was refusing to take criticism and prejudice personally. The second was to expand my qualifications for my career, such as earning a new license or certification, in order to improve my credentials. I still continue to do that today.

What got you through tough times in your career or personal life?

I have the belief that difficult times pass sooner or later. I believe in focusing on a positive future outcome. On my office computer I have a quote from Albert Camus that says: "In the depth of winter, I found in me an invincible summer."

What's essential for having a successful career?

If you are not a whole person, a happy and content person, then your career does not matter. Respect your personal life; take time for it and don't feel that you are detracting from your efforts at work by doing so. The more joy you have in your private life, the better your performance will be at work.

Jan Marini

President and CEO of skincare company Jan Marini Skin Research, Inc.

What advice would you give to women who want to follow in your footsteps?

The only way that anything is ever accomplished or fully realized is by taking action. You can discuss an idea, endlessly plan and try to predetermine whether or not you will be successful, but, while it is essential to have an overall vision, focus and tenacity, reaching your goal ultimately hinges on jumping in and relentlessly moving forward.

What's the best way to stay focused at work?

Always compete with yourself, not the competition. If you're constantly using other people as the yardstick to measure your success, you're not putting your energy and passion where it belongs. You're the only person who can determine how successful you will be.

How can you have a successful personal life?

Give it the respect you give to your business. If you want to be successful and joyful in your personal relationships, communicate, generously give recognition, inspire, motivate, and love fiercely and with all your heart. When I am working, I am intensely focused and in the moment. When I am with my husband, I am just as intensely focused on him and enriching our relationship.

Karen Dee

President and CEO of Fifth Third Bank (Central Florida affiliate).

What advice would you give to women who want to follow in your footsteps?

Find a mentor early in your career and, as time goes on, give back by being a mentor to someone else. And raise your hand when opportunities arise. Make it known you are interested. Be your own PR agent; know that it's OK to talk about your accomplishments. Also, highlighting the team around you is a good way to highlight yourself.

What's the most important thing to remember when it comes to your career?

Gain experiences, not jobs. All the while you'll be learning something new and building transferable skills.

What's the biggest career mistake you've made?

Believing that performance mattered more than relationships with people. It's critical in hiring to be sure that individuals are a cultural and motivational fit to the organization. It's all about the people.

Lori Greiner

Started a $400 million organizing brand with over 250 products sold on QVC.

What gets you through tough times in your career?

Knowing that I have the ability to fix things and to turn a situation around. I always try to look at the bright side of a bad situation and see what I can learn from it. Remember, there is not always just one path to follow. Sometimes you may need to take a circuitous path to get to the same end.

How do you balance your career and your personal life?

I have it easy because my husband works with me. I highly recommend this. It is great to work as a team toward achieving the same goal. I think you also remain very close because you are able to share all aspects of your life together in a very all-encompassing way.

How did you overcome your biggest career hurdle?

My biggest career hurdle was getting my products into retail. It's very difficult for a little company with just one product to get into mass retail. But if your product is good, people will recognize this and see its merits. Be passionate and find creative ways to get your product in front of the decision makers. And don't give up, I must have called 100 times to get hold of some buyers before I finally reached them.

Michelle Edelman

President of Solana Beach, California, advertising agency NYCA.

How do you balance your career and your personal life?

Women often quit good jobs seeking "work-life balance" when really, you have to give work-life balance as a gift to yourself and it's a challenge and a decision every day. No job is going to help you assure you're there for the important moments in your family's life. You have the power to do this for yourself through being organized, knowing what you want and figuring out what is and isn't important to get ahead in your job.

How can being a woman help in terms of a career?

It's said the pay gap is now closing for women, but there's still a pay divide. That said, women are being hired at a faster rate than men right now. I think in the recovery economy, women have tremendous opportunity to flex their career muscle. By being the less expensive option, you can go for a job that pushes you ahead and use the pay gap as an advantage over the "pricier" guy colleague.

To what do you attribute your success?

Even in my field, which is replete with creative women, it's rare to find a woman in management. There's no way I would be if I didn't have tremendous support from my husband. Most women, even though qualified to rise in companies, don't because they really can't organize their lives to support that rise.

Laura Torrado, DDS, FAGD

Dentist with her own Manhattan practice who has been donating dental reconstruction work to victims of domestic violence, hate crimes and poor healthcare for eight years.

What's the key to reaching your goals?

Keeping my final goal in mind and establishing personal timelines: What do I want to achieve and by when? Am I willing to go through the necessary steps to get it done? It helps to write them down and break them into smaller goals and achievements to lead toward a greater end.

What do you know now that you wish you had known when you were younger?

There are ways to raise money to open your own business. External financing will get you off the ground and going without having to wait for years before you have the capital to get started. A good business plan presented to a lender in your field will probably give you what you need. Women are a "minority" and with that in mind, we have access to more resources. Just be savvy and find them. If you believe your business is truly a great idea, you should easily be able to convince others of the same thing.

If you could change anything about your career path or life, what would it be?

I would change the motto that "the client is always right." This is not true. Trying to please everybody can be a futile exercise in business and in your personal life. In the end you won't have the results you were hoping for. To compromise for the sake of compromise really leaves you with a bad taste in your mouth. Define who you are and what you want to achieve and stick to it. Always be yourself, everybody else is taken!

"I believe confident women are world changers."

— Lauren Freeman

Your Personal Study Guide Notes:

_____

_____

_____

_____

_____

_____

_____

_____

_____

_____

_____

_____

_____

_____

_____

_____

_____

_____

_____

_____

_____

_____

13

Cosmetics and Beauty

Fresh, Natural Makeup

FOR A FABULOUS face, strive for a clean and natural look in your makeup. The comment you want to hear is, "You look fabulous." If the comment is about your makeup, you're wearing too much. The natural look is not as innocent as it appears. It takes time, skills and know-how. The trick is in learning the fundamentals of makeup application—to blend, brush smooth and blend some more, until all lines disappear. Blend until the colors become part of your face and the look is naturally beautiful and fabulous!

Makeup

- **Foundation:** *The purpose of makeup foundation is to even out your skin color. If you put it on and can't see it—that's your color!*

- **Coverstick:** *May be used under foundation to even out unusually dark discolorations on your face. For example, dark circles around eyes or red and purple discolorations. Blend carefully with the fingers.*

- **Powder:** *Dust on lightly to prevent clinging and remove excess with cotton.*

- **Cheek Blush:** *The purpose of cheek blush is to give your face a fresh look of vitality and health.*

- **Lipstick Lipcolor:** *Creates a pretty mouth and softens, protects and moisturizes lips. Makeup foundation applied under lipstick can make lip color last longer. Apply Lipcolor with a lipbrush for a professional look.*

- **Lipliner:** *Use a lipbrush to sketch a correction in your Lipliner, with the brush fill in the color all the way to the corners of your mouth. It's a good idea to seek a professional's help with sketching a correction.*

- **Lip Gloss:** *Do not use lip gloss under lipstick.*

- **Eye Shadow:** *Should emphasize eyes, not the shadow, blend carefully, pick transparent colors, and don't overdo.*

- **Eyeliner:** *For a fresh, natural makeup look, eye makeup needs to be applied sparingly or not used at all. Eyeliner is used to define and enhance eye shape.*

- **Eyebrows:** *Hold a pencil vertically alongside the nose. Brows should begin over the inner corner of the eye where the pencil touches the brow.*

- *Mascara: Apply mascara using a mascara wand; brush a thin coat of color from root of your lashes to tip of each lash. Keep lashes combed apart with an eyelash comb, allow to dry.*

Tips

Remember that makeup is not a complete look. It is part of your total look and should blend with clothes in color. Set your makeup table with water and moisturizer, mirror, cotton swabs as erasers for mistakes, cotton balls for dusting on powder. Buy good quality makeup tools, good sponges, soft, sable brushes, etc. They will last longer and help you with blending your makeup for soft, natural and fabulous look.

Less expensive makeup is not necessarily of poorer quality. Cosmetics are required to meet standards set by the Federal Drug Administration. Makeup alone will not create a fresh, fabulous, new look a new image must include a new hairstyle. Don't be afraid to change with the times. A look that was popular ten or twenty years ago dates our appearance. Change is exciting!

Consult fashion magazines for ideas for fresh, new and fabulous wholesome makeup ideas. Consult a department store makeup artist who has been trained by a makeup company. The makeup artist can help you make decisions about colors best for you. Makeup is not only an instant beautifier and morale-builder, it's fun and fabulous!

- *Change is the best morale booster one can experience.*
- *Coordinate your cheek blush color to your lip color.*
- *Your makeup table should be in good light.*
- *Take your time. If you don't have time to apply makeup well, don't wear it at all.*
- *Check your daytime makeup in bright daylight and recheck it during the day to be sure it still looks fabulous and fresh.*

- *Give yourself time to adjust to a change you are trying to make. Our faces are the last place we will make a change.*

Image and Body Investment

FASHION CAN BE BOUGHT.
Style one must possess.

Image

Successful images begin with only you in control of your image. Your effective image is managing self-talk evolved from the past experiences with similar situations. If your experience has been pleasant or good, your self-talk will tend to be positive. If experiences were negative or bad, your self-talk will tend to be negative: How you think, how you feel, how you behave. Be aware of your own self-talk during various situations, know the differences between positive and negative. Manage your self-talk, so that you can affect the outcome based on how dedicated you are on improving your image.

"When you look fabulous, you feel good and confident.
It is a total package!"

— Lauren Freeman

Body Image

Here's how you master the mind that is tagged with body image: Getting to the ideal shape and improving self perception. Take a long, hard look in your mirror, master your self-confidence by getting rid of unrealistic views of beauty, weight loss, and weight gain.

As you can see, accepting your body today won't halt your progress, it will fuel it. And this will help you work toward your ideal shape and not somebody else's. Start creating an amazing fabulous body journey.

Love Your Body

Enjoy loving your body. The truth is that this concept of being grateful for our bodies is essential to getting fit and staying fit. Loving your body enough to put the time and effort into it, this is where every successful health, fitness, and weight loss program begins. Understanding your image, allows you as an individual, to gain confidence in yourself, and your journey towards a fabulous you, begins now.

Body Truth

It can be hard to offer three cheers to the mirror when you don't feel your best. But think about this: How on earth will you start taking better care of your body if you hate it? Women tell me how they're not totally pleased with what they see in the mirror, but the truth is that our bodies are miraculous. They do so many amazing things for us. Love what you see and make your fabulous journey fun. Why not try doing what apes do in front of the mirror? They "groom themselves, pick food out of their teeth and make faces at themselves for entertainment," according to the Social Issues Research Centre. Doesn't that sound like more fun than our pessimistic reflections?

The Mind

When you begin the fabulous mind journey toward your ideal shape, it's really important to understand the connection between the mirror, your mind, and your body. Negativity will close the door to weight loss, while positivity will swing it wide open. It is hard to be upbeat about our bodies at the outset of the program, but we have to. Not only will pessimism hinder progress, it may even be the cause of weight gain or weight fluctuation. Mood imbalances like guilt, depression, anger, and stress are often contributing factors in weight management issues.

Body Connection

We have found that weight loss hypnotherapy is an incredible tool for correcting negative thoughts and habits. It helps people learn to tune out deconstructive messages from the media, our culture, people in our lives, and our own subconscious minds. By incorporating hypnotherapy into your weight loss program, you can make healthy choices because you love your body and you love the results. This is so much more effective than trying to improve your body while punishing yourself and being critical.

Better Body

Imagine how you could look better, because you have mastered the mirror and learned to love your body at every stage of weight loss. Recognizing the positive things about your body today will improve your perception of you and will give more confidence to succeed in every aspect of your life's fabulous journey of weight loss.

> *"Nothing is more fabulous then looking tall, sexy, sophisticated, your new improved, healthy and mirrored body, be passionate about your journey. Change is a fact of life and your body type is changing all the time. Know your new fabulous and healthy body. Own it!"*

— Lauren Freeman

Your Personal Study Guide Notes:

_____

_____

_____

_____

_____

_____

_____

_____

_____

_____

_____

_____

_____

_____

_____

_____

_____

_____

_____

_____

_____

_____

_____

14

Fashion and Style

Women's Dress Fit Guide

USE THESE TIPS to identify your body shape and find the most flattering fit and the dresses that are best for your body.

Little definition between bust, waist, and hip measurements

Fitted sheaths and classic shifts work well with your shape, while an Empire waist or a simple A-line skirt helps to create some curves. One-shoulder styles ensure a dramatic silhouette.

Fuller at the hips and rear and smaller on top

Dresses with fitted open-neck or strapless tops enhance your upper body and draw the eye up, while full or A-line skirts help hide wider hips. An Empire waist marks the smallest point of your figure, distracting from everything else.

Curvaceous, with full bust, defined waist and full hips

Wraps, knit dresses and classic sheaths with fitted waists enhance your classically feminine form. Look for adjustable-waist styles for the best fit.

Narrowest point is above the natural waist; at the ribs

Empire waists draw the eye up, taking attention away from the middle and allowing a looser fit. Neck details also bring the focus up, while full skirts and A-line shifts create an hourglass illusion.

Bust measurement is fuller than hips and rear

Classic V-neck wraps and halter styles draw the eye downward for a slimming effect. A-line styles, full skirts and details at the hem help balance out the bottom half.

Fashion is not something that exists in dresses only. Fashion is in the sky, in the street, Fashion has to do with ideas, the way we live, what is happening.

— Coco Chanel

Your Figure

How you live can be hazardous to your health. You hear those discouraging words everywhere, from mom, dad, husband, your friends, even the nightly news! What is a lady to do? A good place to begin is by understanding what a healthy lifestyle is and then plan to make changes where you need to. Eat a nutritious diet because nutritious foods build a healthy and strong body. Exercise! Make your body strong, look and feel good.

Rest

Get enough sleep, take time to yourself, smell the flowers, get out of the normal routine, work in the yard, go for a long walk in the park or the shopping mall.

Relax

Keep a positive outlook on life. Renew your spirit by reading something refreshing and wholesome or by spending time with cheerful friends or family. Don't let unkind people get you down and get in your head. Use your mind and your quiet time to think about the good things in your life.

What is a Nutritious Diet?

Again, after years of research, I'm convinced that we all need many different nutrients to grow and stay healthy. These include vitamins, minerals, protein, fat, and carbohydrates. Different nutrients are found in different types of food. A variety of foods from each of the pyramid food groups every day is important to get the right balance of nutrients. I'm fifty-three years of age. I started working out at the age of fourteen, eating healthy and balanced meals daily and I'm still going strong due to my healthy lifestyle. It works!

The Food Guide Pyramid and Its Pieces

The pyramid is an outline of what to eat each day. It's a general guide that lets you choose a healthful diet that's right for you! The food guide pyramid emphasizes foods from the five food groups shown in the lower sections of the pyramid. Each of these provides some, but not all of the nutrients you need. Foods in one group can't replace those in another. No one food group is more important than another. For good health you need them all. I recommend learning more about these food groups.

Foods in the Fast Lane

Good news, you don't have to give up eating fast foods. You can eat right and still eat fast foods. I have put a list of fast food for you as a guide.

Here are some tips on fast foods to choose

- *Order a small hamburger instead of a larger one. Try the extra lean hamburger.*
- *Order roast beef for a leaner choice than most burgers.*

- *Order a baked potato instead of French fries. Be careful of high-fat toppings like sour cream or cheese.*

- *Order grilled, broiled, or baked fish and chicken.*

- *Order skim or 1 percent milk instead of a shake. Try the low-fat frozen yogurt.*

- *Order a salad. Use vinegar and oil or low-calorie dressing more often than creamy salad dressing.*

- *Try to create a salad at the salad bar. Choose any raw vegetables, fruits, or beans. Limit high saturated fat toppings like cheese, fried noodles, and some salads made with mayonnaise. Also limit salad dressings high in saturated fat and cholesterol.*

- *For sandwich toppings, try lettuce, tomato and onion, pickles, mustard, and ketchup instead of high saturated fat toppings like cheese, special sauces, or butter.*

- *Order pizza with vegetable toppings like peppers, mushrooms, or onions instead of extra cheese, turkey pepperoni or turkey sausage.*

"Eat to Live. Don't Live to Eat. Be Strong, Be Smart, Stop consuming foods that are not necessarily the healthiest choices for your body. Our bodies need BALANCED MEALS... Eat to Live!"

— Lauren Freeman

Your Personal Study Guide Notes:

_____

_____

_____

_____

_____

_____

_____

_____

_____

_____

_____

_____

_____

_____

_____

_____

_____

_____

_____

_____

Some Suggestions If You Are Overweight

Ladies, this is a tough one. However, we must start somewhere. Why not start now? Condition yourself to move your body faster. Studies done on the same type of lady show that at desired weight, she moves more quickly than when she is carrying too much. Thin ladies move faster, helping to keep their weight down because they are expending more calories. Because being heavy sometimes makes you more inactive, the pounds feel free to accumulate. What I recommend is to keep fresh fruits and fresh vegetables prepared and waiting for snack time so you won't reach for cookies, candy or donuts. Try carrots, cauliflower, celery, broccoli, avocados, apples, peaches, and other fresh fruits with a delicious low-fat dip and organic beverage.

Note that diet pies, candies, cakes, cookies, and junk food are conspicuous only by their absence!

As a rule, the problem of being overweight lies in food versus activity. Too much food and too little activity, your weight goes up and down. You need to balance yourself right in the middle. The big decision! You will make lots of little decisions to lose weight. Once you make *the* decision, it will happen!

Some Suggestions If You Are Too Thin

Eat slowly, eat more at mealtime. Do eat all three meals. Have a nice big snack at bedtime. Lift weights. Get with training to help with this.

Why Should You Exercise

If part of your life means being fresh, healthy and graceful, exercise will help, because exercise improves blood circulation and tones muscles. You will naturally have clearer skin, brighter eyes, fewer illnesses, lots more energy and enthusiasm, and you won't be boring your friends with, "Oh, I'm so tired today" or "My back hurts."

Exercise, Without It, Nutrition Doesn't Help

Promise yourself some mild exercise each and every day. Set goals; create an opportunity for walking every day. Walking is not as strenuous as running, bicycling, or swimming and it involves almost no risk to health for ladies who may have health problems. Walking is good exercise for the legs, heart, and lungs. You will be surprised once you start how easy it gets. Start today. Park your car some distance so you will have to walk. Walk a flight of stairs instead of taking the elevator. Breathe deeply. Life itself depends on oxygen! And inhale and exhale through your nose.

Confidence Exercise

Make yourself look the part that you want. This does not mean going on crazy diets and devoting your whole life to making yourself look good. Just remember to eat healthy, whole foods, exercise, get proper rest, and make yourself look more than merely presentable. Self-confidence makes every woman feel and look more beautiful and fabulous.

Be Active, Exercise

Below are examples of different kinds of exercise that you can do by yourself or with a group of friends. Doing these exercises for fifteen to thirty minutes at least three days a week can help keep your heart and you strong.

Exercise on your Own

- *Bicycling*
- *Brisk Walking*
- *Dancing*
- *Jogging*
- *Jumping Rope*

- *Rollerblading*
- *Running*
- *Skating*

Exercise with Some Friends

- *Baseball and Softball*
- *Basketball*
- *Cross Country Skiing*
- *Football*
- *Frisbee*
- *Gymnastics*
- *Hiking and Backpacking*
- *Ice and Field Hockey*
- *Racquetball*
- *Rowing*
- *Soccer*
- *Swimming*
- *Tennis*

Your Personal Study Guide Notes:

_____

_____

_____

_____

_____

_____

_____

_____

_____

_____

_____

_____

_____

_____

_____

_____

_____

_____

_____

_____

_____

_____

_____

Calm Your Mind & Strengthen Your Body

Start Yoga, Health, and Wellness Journey

The Yoga journey focuses on the connection to the breath, mindful movement, releasing tension, stretching, and relaxing tight joints. Whether you're looking to slow down from a hectic day or looking for a calmer, more mindful practice, a class is perfect for someone seeking a slower pace with emphasis on alignment, balance and breathing practices. Ease tension and increase flexibility and strength in your body while also preparing yourself for some of our more challenging classes and understanding techniques to access intermediate poses.

Yoga Style Mind and Body Classes

- *Hot Yoga: A dynamic and strong class offered in a heated room of 90 to 93 degree Fahrenheit. The heated space will open the muscle tissues. Movement created through physically demanding sequences toward peak poses. The practice will allow the muscles to open, building stamina, detoxifying the body, creating more flexibility, and centering of breath for steadiness. This class is recommended for the seasoned practitioner.*

- *Restore Yu: Through the use of props and breath, you will find stillness and ease in your body and mind. All poses are recline, supine, prone, and seated asana. Poses are held for five to seven minutes each and move you through seventy-five minutes of stress-relieving, calmly guided instruction. All we ask you to do is let go and completely relax.*

- *Yu Flow: Our description of vinyasa-style yoga with beautiful and creative sequence connecting each asana in flow with music and mindful breath. The practice will take you from heart opening posture to forward bends, warrior poses, and*

Sun Salutations, to name a few. Find flow and open your body is the mindful yogic practice.

- **Yu Rise:** *A perfect way to start the day as you awaken the body and mind at our earliest class of the day. Experience the powerful benefits of your practice as you also stretch and tone your body. This is an all-level class that sets the intention for the remainder of your day.*

- **Beginner Yoga:** *This class focuses on the foundation of yoga, integrating breath with asana (poses). Demonstration of form and alignment are key to creating confidence and a safe, but positive experience.*

- **Yu Sculpt and Tone:** *A class designed for all levels integrating weights, bolster, and yoga poses. Emphasis is placed on yoga poses building upper body strength with light weights, core yoga, gluteus, and quadriceps workouts blending yoga poses and flexibility.*

- **Power 4Yu:** *One of our stronger classes that integrate upper body strength, flow, and longer holding poses. The practice will open and flow to ultimately move toward a stronger alignment of poses. Core yoga, planks along with intermediate poses will be incorporated throughout the practice.*

Pick an activity that is fun to do by yourself or with friends. Plan a skating party or pack a picnic and take a day hike, throw a dance party, join a sports team. It all adds up to a more healthy, fabulous you! Promise yourself to plan an activity, invite friends and join a girls' night out group! Do it now!

Tips

Look in the mirror to start convincing yourself to learn new and better eating habits and to exercise regularly. Take time and effort. It's worth it. Don't be an excuse maker. Stay with it, you might find it hard in the beginning, but when you start to see and feel results, it might even get to be fun, I've been exercising since I was fourteen, I work out three days a week for two hours. It's just part of my lifestyle, like brushing your teeth or your hair!

Look Ten Pounds Thinner

One of the easiest ways to look ten pounds thinner is to wear clothing that fits well. Two of the biggest fashion mistakes which can add pounds are wearing oversized, baggy clothing, and wearing clothing that is too tight. Although achieving a great fit can be difficult, especially for petite women and sometimes may require some clothing alterations, great fitting clothing will make any woman look thinner.

Oversized Clothing Makes for an Oversized Appearance

Clothing that's very loose, baggy, or saggy gives the illusion that the wearer is even bigger than she really is. So although it's tempting to wear oversized garments in an attempt to conceal a few extra pounds, this strategy doesn't work for the woman who wants to look thinner. For example a single-breasted, well-fitting tailored jacket with a nipped-in waist or vertical seam lines will visually take off pounds, but a long, loose, oversized, shapeless jacket will add pounds.

Tight Clothing Reveals Figure Flaws

Tight clothing not only reveals figure flaws that can easily be concealed with well-cut clothing that fits properly, but it also makes a woman look bigger than she really is. A jacket worn open because it can't be buttoned, jeans that are almost impossible to zip, tops that are so tight they restrict arm movement, and horizontal wrinkles across the bust or hips are all signs that clothing is too tight, so any woman who wants to look thinner should avoid too-tight clothing.

Too often, we're tempted to squeeze into clothing that's too small because of that little number on the tag. You know the one, it's the size. Getting hung up on a certain size, no matter whether it's a size 0 or a size 20 and refusing to wear any clothing labeled with a larger size frequently gets women into trouble with clothing fit. There's no law that says you have to leave the size tag in any article of clothing after you purchase it, so if that irritating size tag really bugs you, simply remove it before you wear the garment and congratulate yourself for having chosen a garment that truly fits.

Your Personal Study Guide Notes:

_____

_____

_____

_____

_____

_____

_____

_____

_____

_____

_____

_____

_____

_____

_____

_____

_____

_____

_____

_____

_____

_____

_____

_____

15

Having Streams
of Awareness

Medical Check for Women

SHOULD YOU GET an annual physical? Here's what you need to know. The annual physical came under fire recently when a medical study suggested it was no longer necessary. The news, combined with recent changes in cancer screening guidelines, left many people confused. How often should you see your doctor for checkups to stay healthy?

There's no one-size-fits-all answer, says Heidi Doyle, PA-C, a physician assistant North Hills Internal Medicine, a Duke Primary Care clinic. "Regular check-ups are important to maintain a relationship with your doctor and to receive individualized counseling based on your family health history and your lifestyle."

Age and disease risk are the primary factors influencing when to get a physical, says Doyle.

With this in mind, here's what you need to know:

- *If you're under thirty and healthy, don't smoke, no disease risk factors (including being overweight), and don't take prescription medications, get a check-up every two to three years. If you're a woman and sexually active, get a Pap smear to screen for cervical cancer starting at age twenty-one and discuss how often you should screen with your provider.*

- *Age thirty to forty, healthy individuals should get a physical every other year. Baseline mammograms are now recommended for women once they turn forty and should be repeated every one to two years.*

- *Annual physicals start around age fifty. That's also when men and women should undergo colonoscopies to screen for colon cancer. Repeat every ten years unless there is a family history of colon cancer, colon polyps or the test results are abnormal.*

- *Different recommendations about check-up frequency apply to individuals who take medication and have chronic disease risk factors. In that case, annual physicals may be recommended since blood tests may be necessary and treatments may need to be changed.*

- *Being overweight also influences how often you get a physical because it increases one's risk for high blood pressure, high cholesterol and diabetes. "For these individuals, the annual physical is an opportunity to reinforce healthy lifestyle choices," Doyle says.*

- *"The key is for each person to be responsible for their own health," says Doyle. A person with diabetes, high blood pressure or high cholesterol, or one who is simply more susceptible to those conditions, can make lifestyle changes that are much more impactful than any pill I can prescribe."*

Everyone can make the most of their physical if they heed this advice, says Doyle.

Arrive on Time

- *Know the names and doses of any medications you are taking, including over-the-counter supplements.*

- *Bring your vaccine record including when you received your last flu shot-annual, tetanus-every ten years, and pertussis-in the last ten years.*

- *Bring the dates of your last cancer screenings.*

- *Be honest. Be honest. Being truthful about your smoking and or drinking habits gives the doctor the information she needs to provide the appropriate counseling to maximize your health.*

Written by Staff for Duke Medicine | Added February 6, 2014

An annual exam is part of your health care. If it has been more than twelve months, please contact your health care provider to schedule an exam.

What is an annual exam? An annual exam is a once-a-year visit to your primary care provider for a general health check, including a breast exam and Pap smear. An annual exam visit does not include discussion of new problems or detailed review of chronic conditions. Annual exams are also called routine check-up, yearly exam, annual Pap, and preventive.

Please schedule a separate appointment if you have health concerns other than your routine physical exam.

Examples

- *A list of concerns or questions*
- *New health care concerns or problems found at the time of your annual exam*
- *Ongoing health problems that need more attention*

What should I expect during my annual exam?

- *General physical exam (including breast exam)*
- *Pelvic exam (pap smear)*
- *Update of life and work situation*
- *Update of family health history (any new serious illnesses in your family?)*
- *Review of your health history*
- *Update of current medications, herbs and supplements (bring list)*
- *Need for medication refills*
- *Evaluation of need for health screening tests based on age and personal and family history (such as mammogram, test for sexually transmitted diseases and colon cancer screening)*
- *Update on immunizations*

What happens if you have a new health problem when you come for your annual exam?

You and your provider will need to decide whether to use the time that day to address your problem, in which case your annual exam visit can be rescheduled. Or you may choose to go ahead with your annual exam and to defer the health concern to another visit. Scheduled appointment times do not allow for both.

Primary Care Provider (PCP)

- *Please check your insurance policy to make sure you are covered for yearly preventive medicine visits or women's health pap/pelvic/breast exam. Different insurance policies have different rules for preventive care coverage.*

- *Most insurance companies allow for only one annual exam per twelve-month period and some will not pay for a visit even a few days before your policy is up.*

Insurance Coverage Issues

- *Please check your insurance policy to make sure you are covered for yearly preventive medicine visits or women's health pap/pelvic/breast exam. Different insurance policies have different rules for preventive care coverage.*
- *Most insurance companies allow for only one annual exam per twelve-month period (and some will not pay for a visit even a few days before your policy is up).*

Medicare Issues

- *Medicare covers Paps every two years, mammograms every year, colon cancer screening, and routine vaccinations.*
- *If you are considered high risk, Medicare will pay for annual Pap smears.*
- *Medicare does not cover routine annual exams. You may choose to pay for routine physicals and tests out-of-pocket.*

According to Dr. Roshini Raj, as you get older, your health needs change. Are you and your doctor keeping up? From STD tests to colonoscopies, here are the most important health tests for women, according to Dr. Roshini Raj, TODAY contributor and medical editor for Health magazine.

Women's Physical

- *Twenties: Complete physical.*
- *Twenty-one: Get your first physical at age twenty-one, then once every five years until age forty.*

- *Forty: You should start getting a yearly physical. Make sure to get checks on your blood sugar, cholesterol, thyroid function, liver/kidney function, vitamin B12 and vitamin D.*

More On Health

- *FDA knew of problems at plant that made tainted wipes.*
- *Big drop seen in ear infections. Say what.*
- *Could Sheen really kick addiction with his mind?*
- *Diet rules that don't suck.*
- *FOX's anchor Why I'm talking about infertility.*
- *12 tips for easing your 'parent-noia'*
- *Better with age? Midlife crises are a myth.*

Tests

- **Pap Test:** *This test can spot the earliest signs of cervical cancer, when the chance of curing it is very high.*
- **Get the Pap Test:** *At your yearly gyno exam, starting at age twenty-one. At age thirty, if you've had three consecutive normal results, you may only need a Pap every three years until age sixty-five.*
- **STD Tests:** *Of the nineteen million new STD infections each year, almost half of them are between fifteen- to twenty-four-year-olds. If left untreated, some of these can lead to infertility down the road. Get tested annually for HIV, Chlamydia, and Gonorrhea when you become sexually active (or when you're starting a new relationship).*
- **Skin Check:** *Melanoma is the leading cause of cancer death for women ages twenty-five to twenty-nine. The incidence among young women has increased by 50 percent over the last thirty years (largely due to the use of tanning beds). See*

a dermatologist annually if you have a family history of skin cancer or semi-annually if you have actually had the disease.

In your 30s

- **HPV Test:** *HPV is the leading cause of cervical cancer and most sexually active women get the infection at some point. Beginning around age thirty, women become more prone to infection because our immune systems are less robust. Get the test at age thirty and then with your Pap every three years if results are normal.*

- **Blood Sugar Test:** *Anything above normal should be checked out, so the doctor can intervene before it becomes full-blown diabetes. Get tested every three years until you turn fifty, when you should be tested annually (the risk of diabetes increases significantly with age).*

In your 40s

Cholesterol Test: *Start getting physicals annually at 40 and include this test particularly if you smoke or have high blood pressure, diabetes or family history of heart disease.*

In your 50s

- **Mammogram:** *The overall risk of getting breast cancer increases with age between ages fifty and fifty-nine, 1 in 42 women are likely to develop it. This number climbs to 1 in every 29 for women aged sixty to sixty-nine. Early detection and treatment help prevent the spread of the disease and boost your odds of recovery. Get one every two years.*

- **In your 50s:** *Colonoscopy: Go in for the procedure at age fifty, then every ten years to screen for colorectal cancer, the second* *leading killer in the US among all cancers. Adults fifty and over run the highest risk of developing the disease, but studies show that people who get a colonoscopy every ten years have better outcomes if they do develop cancer.*

Your Personal Study Guide Notes:

_____

_____

_____

_____

_____

_____

_____

_____

_____

_____

_____

_____

_____

_____

_____

_____

_____

_____

_____

_____

_____

_____

_____

16

Score Lauren's Fabulous Lifestyle

WE ARE EXCITED to share our Fabulous Lifestyle "Boot Camp 101" training programs, our plans, and approach with you.

Fabulous boot camp staff (FBCS) knows that life can be overwhelming, so with you in mind, we promise to attempt at every goal set to be met. With our programs, we offer professional image programs that are award winning with solid expert advice from Lauren Freeman, the founder, style icon, and her team of brand ambassadors, style experts, image trainers, and top leaders in the fashion industry. FBCS experts will provide training with a proven track record, high-quality and BIG results. This will include information on how to master the mirror and embrace the new and more confident you. Enjoy Networking while style swapping, discover new looks, new friendships, and more.

Camp 101 style is renowned for helping a new generation of individuals, learn how to create their individual brand. Learn to shop and style on a dime. This training is for like-minded women.

Score Boot Camp 101 Training

- *Image Training*
- *Image Consultant*
- *Fashion Stylist*
- *Color Consultant*
- *Personal Shopper*
- *Wardrobe Stylist*
- *Business Image*

Score a Lifestyle Boot Camp 101

- *Fashion*
- *Health*
- *Fitness*
- *Beauty*
- *Businesss*
- *Entertainment*
- *Décor*

Score a Fabulous Closet Makeover

- *Dealing with Sentimental Clutter*
- *How to Organize Your Closet*
- *Ways to Eliminate Clutter*

Cash in on Your Closet Today

- *Alert your closet*
- *Fashion style and style and trends*
- *NEW confidence & sense of style*
- *Swapping uncovers NEW looks & friendships!*

Flip Your Closet, Get Rid of Your Old Clothes

It might not be easy, but tossing out or donating old clothes is key to making room in your closet. My belief is to donate anything you haven't worn in more than two years. Also, if it's two sizes too small or two sizes too big, get rid of it. It's time to buy new clothes. Ask yourself if you would buy this item today or if it has a sentimental factor that warrants storage.

Call the Pros

If you're interested in hiring professional help to organize your closet, it may be more affordable than you think. A custom closet is a luxury that many of us can afford. Even the major closet companies can design what you would like on a budget, but if that is not an option, I suggest using storage units that allow you to see your clothes and accessories. If you can't see it, you don't wear it! If you have the space to hang everything, hang everything; you'll wear more if you can see it. The Container Store provides some excellent items. Use SlimLine Hangers. Your clothes won't fall off and they'll give you twice the space of plastic.

Start Organizing

How do you organize sweaters versus lingerie or shoes versus jeans? There are different solutions for each, so you can start de-cluttering your closet.

Sweaters

Fold the very heavy sweaters so they don't lose shape on the hanger. Also, cedar is not a myth. It really does prevent moths from getting into your cashmere or wool sweaters. Replace the cedar every six months. Use dividers or cubbies. Use a sweater folding board to make perfect folds. Cedar or lavender scented folding boards.

Jeans

How you want to organize your jeans is a personal choice. There are a number of ways to do so by cut, brand, color, style, size, or none of the above. I tend to go by color I just prefer it that way unless they're die-hard jeans collectors. I hang by the hem and organize by dark to light denim.

Pants | Skirts | Shorts

How to hang pants, skirts and shorts: Hang them using clips and fold in the sides so the outside of the garment isn't marked by the clips. This also makes everything look uniform on the hanger and gives it a cleaner side profile in your closet.

Dresses

For dresses, I recommend hanging by color rather than length. I also like to start with strapless and go to long-sleeve. Never leave your dresses, or any other clothes, in the dry cleaning or plastic garment bags. The chemicals from dry cleaning attack the fibers of your clothing and cause damage. Choose to divide dresses by length but also season and day or night.

Bags | Scarves | Hats

I like purses out of their dust bags and to have as many visible as possible. It's hard to change bags if you can't see them. They don't generally get damaged out of their dust bags, so enjoy the view. Scarves folded in piles by color and material works best and makes it easy to pull one out without ruining the organization of the rest. For hats, I love hat boxes. Take uniform photos of the hats and glue them to the outside of the boxes.

Shoes

I prefer shoes to go right shoe toe out and left shoe heel out so you can see both to make finding what you're planning to wear easy. Organize shoes by color and style. I always hide tennis shoes and flip-flops in the least seen place.

Lingerie

Organize by color, size and type. Make sure to rotate your bras and underwear so you're not wearing the same few all of the time. For a luxe and fabulous touch, I line drawers in silk and sometimes do sachet-lined drawers.

Accessories

If you have room in your wardrobe, hang your necklaces (color coded and in the same length) on jewelry or accessory hooks. If they're in a drawer, you might not see them and therefore you won't wear them.

Jewelry

I am partial to a built-in drawer in one's closet or dresser in order to keep things neat and uncluttered. It's also a great way to see what you have and makes it easy to keep hidden from plain sight.

Tips: Proper Hangers

Proper clothing care calls for appropriate hangers, satin padding for more delicate items and sturdy wood hangers for tailored jackets.

> *"Nothing excites me more than an organized beautiful closet."*
>
> — Lauren Freeman

Score A Big Boost of Confidence

Fashion boot camp will show you how to boost your confidence, snag more compliments, and attract more opportunities.

Health Food Revolution

Use your favorite search engine and add these links for valuable information regarding health food.

- *The Ultimate Body Weight Loss*
- *Fitness Specialist and Nutritionist*
- *Weight Loss Solution*
- *Combination of Clean Eating*
- *Weight Training and Cardio*
- *New Body*

- *The New Life You Deserve*
- *Most challenging, stubborn fat can be lost and lives can be changed forever*

Best Boot Camp Group

Use your favorite search engine and add these links for valuable information regarding the best boot camp groups.

- *Best Exercise Trend*
- *Group Fitness*
- *P.E. Style Workouts*
- *Hydro Aerobics in the pool*
- *Body Sculpting*
- *Boxing*
- *Twist on a Spin Class*
- *Real Ryder Bicycles, These super-fun bikes tilt like you're rounding a corner, engaging your abs and leg muscles. Test them out when you take a class.*

Your Personal Study Guide Notes:

_____

_____

_____

_____

_____

_____

_____

_____

_____

_____

_____

_____

_____

_____

_____

_____

_____

_____

_____

_____

_____

_____

_____

_____

_____

17

Membership
"Members Only"

Score Lauren's Fabulous Closets

Flip My Closet

YOU ARE NOW a member and a part of Flip My Closet. Here you'll gain access to covetable items from the closets of the fashionable women around the country and earn money cleaning out your own wardrobe. We hope that Flip My Closet will soon become your destination for discovering beloved pieces and fresh looks.

Score Fabulous Thread Exchange

One of the most popular free and fabulous thread exchange, fashion exchange, all over the world, it's fun, eco-friendly, a way to save money, look fabulous and gorgeous, refresh your closet, while giving back and passing it on! A recent study by Goodwill Industries found that 23.8 billion pounds of clothing and textiles end up in Untied States landfills every year! And that is just in the Untied States alone. Offers an alternative that's healthy for the planet and your bank bank account. We like to call it "guilt-free thread exchange shopping." It feels so good to us to help women save money and the planet at the same time passing it on!

Score Style-Swap

Just to give you an idea or two, every piece of clothing you don't want, bring to the event to swap! So for best results, you need to bring ten to fifteen pieces of clothing that you've been photographed in and are tired of wearing. Note that all pieces should be clean and ready to wear only!

Fabulous Diva's Movement

Fabulous Diva's movement and completing this book, it's your gift of learning and my personal invitation for you to become a member.

What's included in your membership:

- *Lifetime Membership.*
- *You will receive my signature tool, called the mirror.*
- *You will also receive a certificate of completion.*
- *Your personal guide notes from each chapter.*
- *A mentor or a brand ambassador.*

- *Advance your personal life and career in your respective industries by creating a brand.*

- *Marketing strategy that houses all facets of fashion, health, wealth and beauty.*

Your Personal Study Guide Notes:

_____

_____

_____

_____

_____

_____

_____

_____

_____

_____

_____

_____

_____

_____

_____

_____

_____

_____

_____

_____

_____

_____

18

Daily Practice

Daily Practice

PRACTICE THIS IN the mirror daily. Practice your smile. Smile when you talk to people. Laughing too loud is against the fabulous rules. Remember to always be a lady, be nice. If you're nice, respectful and want to be liked, you have to be nice and respectful. But of course, it's much better to be liked by people, so being nice and treating others with respect will help. A woman's behavior is to socialize, speak calmly, not monopolizing all the attention. Develop conversation skills.

You can use this as a measure of your sense of self-worth and confidence: If you were dropped in the middle of a daunting social situation, say, the red carpet tomorrow among the most respected, poised and famous leaders, philanthropists, business-women, actresses, designers, etc., would you be comfortable?

Would you believe that you too have something of value to bring to the occasion?

This is about a confidence in you to be able to handle anything that happens. I know this is not easy, because sometimes, we feel very uncertain, vulnerable, lost, unloved, hurt, shocked, and overwhelmed. We all have those moments, but remember, it is what you do about it most of the time (not some of the time) that counts. It really goes back to valuing yourself. Keep practicing, learning and growing while you are on your fabulous journey to a new lifestyle. Practicing daily with your mirror leads to greater results.

Want More Style?

For women wanting more, I recommend to read more fashion magazines and know what's hot and what's not at the moment. You can also create your own style and have your own look. It's not right to wear something that just isn't you. Being you is the way to go. It's often better to have a basic personal style than to always be chasing the latest "fad." In chapter 19 and 20, I have designed a guide for you to take when you go shopping and for notes, during your fabulous journey. You must be true to yourself, so stay true to your feminine core and be okay being a fabulous woman.

Don't view having long hair as a drag. Put the effort into looking pretty and beautiful. Women are supposed to look and more importantly, be attractive, being fabulous, glamorous, whatever it takes. This is only going to happen when you exude the fabulous you, however. It's not about wanting to change what you've been given or being superficial, it's simply about taking pride in your style and your appearance.

Many younger as well as middle-aged women simply let themselves go. In other words, they lost themselves years ago. They start to value themselves less. They get fat, stop combing or styling their hair nicely, stop making the time to exercise, eat well, or socialize.

Know your style

Still not sure about your style? Choose someone you admire and model her style. Ask for help. The best way to start dressing is to choose someone you identify with and see what she wears. Carefully observe the posture on those women!

Red flag appearance

Letting it go can sometimes be a telltale sign that you habitually feel bad about yourself and your life. Or that you don't care about yourself, which negates the fabulous you. Aging is not an issue for a true diva woman. I'm in my fifties and I have several sisters and friends in their fifties. So to us, age can and often does wonderful things for a woman, including giving her added value and beauty! Have fun on your fabulous journey.

Make a Positive Impression

Have good taste in clothing. Be modest in clothing and avoid clothing of bad taste. Extremely low necklines, too short skirts, belly-baring tops, and revealing clothing can make a girl look like she does not respect her body and herself. Shirts with inappropriate sayings, logos or sexual innuendos can make a girl look like she's desperate for attention. My mother would say to her daughters, "Classy ladies are not desperate for attention."

Classy ladies don't talk about sexual immorality. They tend to talk about fashion, but they should also talk about intellectual topics, books, art, politics/current events, and more. Increase your vocabulary and stay away from slang terms. Never slouch. Having good posture is important, yet rare. This is about confidence in yourself to be able to handle anything that happens and comes your way. I know this is not easy, because sometimes, we feel very uncertain, vulnerable, lost, unloved, hurt, shocked, and overwhelmed. We all have those moments, but again remember, it is what you do about it most of the time (not some of the time) that counts.

Never sell yourself, for any amount or anything! Self-respect is the most important thing a woman can have. Be true to yourself and don't let anyone else steer you away from the right path and stop you from achieving your goals. Hold out for your better life! This may sound old fashioned, but it is essential, if you want to fulfill dreams and know your true love and not end up in complicated situations that may cost you your life's best dreams, including your commitment to your true life's love.

These Days, dating seems like a casual activity, but it certainly is not. Settling for a "coin flip" decision on giving yourself away could get you into a lot of complicated situations that will ruin your life! If a guy loves you enough, he will want to spend his entire life with you and he wouldn't mind waiting until marriage (that's if he's the right guy for you). If he is willing to wait for "you," it will really show you that he loves you, not just one more temporary sexual rush. He will have to love you as a person, rather than just appreciating your body. There's a reason for signing up for the long term, totally committed relationship: Your whole life can still be ahead of you, not in a cracked rearview mirror.

Million-Dollar Personality

You are the sum total of your personality, mannerisms, yourself, and your daily walk. If a woman walks around with her shoulders slumped, people subconsciously pick up on this energy. I promise you, they are thinking no personality, self-control, even if they don't consciously know your posture is bad. Make daily, personal, short-term development goals that lead to long term personality and to your life goals. Take action to set you on the pathway to achieve the million-dollar personality. Drop the identity thing and go for the fabulous rules over anything.

More than ever, now it is time for change. People are starting to want what is real. I think we all prefer to be around what is real. In the old days, it was a lot about "show" and keeping "face." Now, things are becoming more transparent. Also, we are sick of living in a fast-paced environment where people are always climbing the corporate ladder, valuing things or money, and we want people to know who we are and who we have become. A successful million-dollar smile, positive mannerisms a woman who pays it forward. Plan daily in the mirror how you want to refine and make yourself better in all facets of life throughout your fabulous journey. Keep in mind, people are highly conscious of your mannerisms. They are highly sensitive to these mannerisms. I have listed personal mannerisms to avoid!

- *Scratching*
- *Blinking*
- *Lip biting or sucking*
- *Ear digging*
- *Picking or rubbing the nose*
- *Sarcasm*
- *Boasting*
- *Domineering attitude*

- *Head scratching*
- *Chewing a toothpick*
- *Looking off into space, inattention*
- *An air of boredom*
- *Glancing at the clock or watch*
- *Shuffling the feet*
- *Quickly voice self-pity*
- *Sighing*
- *Slamming doors or drawers*
- *Twitching*
- *Mumbling*
- *Sucking on teeth*
- *Talking down to someone*
- *Staring*
- *Being Suspicious*
- *Swearing*
- *Giving the conversation a crude twist*
- *Constant repetition of words or phrases*
- *Lifting an eyebrow deprecatingly*

Don't Know What to Wear?

Remember, simple is best. Add one or two killer pieces that will have you feeling great and getting compliments along the way. Wear a great outfit with one or two accessories maximum that pop.

Scarves are so versatile. Scarves have so many uses that it is hard not to have any in your wardrobe. Scarves can act as a tie around your hair in a ponytail or used as a headband style, tied around your neck, used as a belt around your waist, or simply tie to the shoulder strap of your handbag for a flirty look. It is good to have variety. Black and red are my favorites. However, I have some softer colors such as pale pink and patterns like hound's-tooth and polka dots. Tasteful floras are very "in" right now also. The scarf belt goes great with a sexy top and pair of jeans.

Your Personal Study Guide Notes:

_____

_____

_____

_____

_____

_____

_____

_____

_____

_____

_____

_____

_____

_____

_____

_____

_____

_____

_____

_____

_____

_____

_____

_____

_____

_____

19

Shopping

Shopping for Fine Jewelry

Guide for Engagment Ring

Know What You Want to Spend

HAVE A PRICE range in mind. Going in with fairly specific parameters will help your jeweler find the right engagement ring to fit your budget.

What Kind of Jewelry Do You Wear

Are you more

- *Classic*
- *Modern*

- *Feminine*
- *Sophisticated*

Do you wear more

- *Silver*
- *Gold*

Do your pieces tend to be more

- *Delicate*
- *Chunky*
- *Simple*

Use your personal guide notes to help with these preferences and keep in mind when you set out to shop. If you buy something similar to what you already like, you can't go wrong.

Know Your Ring Size

Simple, if you wear rings, trace the inner circle on a piece of paper or press the ring into a bar of soap for an impression. You can also slide it down one of your own fingers and draw a line where it stops. A jeweler can use these measurements to identify the approximate ring size.

Know What Diamond Shape Suits You

Here are a few things to keep in mind when considering shape. You will be wearing this ring 24/7 your married life. It will need to go with everything from jeans to evening wear. If you're uncertain about her shape preference, it's sensible to stick to the classics. They became classics because they appeal to most people most of the time.

- *Shapes with fewer facets, such as emerald or square, require higher clarity. The fewer the facets, the more visible any inclusions will be.*

- *Certain shapes pair more successfully with other gems in multistone rings. Round, oval and marquise all work well. Pear and heart shapes are more challenging.*

- *Taste in shape is often reflected in other tastes a woman has. If she prefers clean, modern lines in furniture, for example, it's likely she'll react well to the same aesthetic in emerald or square shapes. If she tends toward the traditional a round shape rarely misses. More bohemian types tend to favor more unusual shapes, like trillian or marquise.*

What Setting Makes Sense

While there are an unending variety of patterns, details and metal choices, there are four basic types you are likely to encounter.

- **Solitaire:** *A single stone. Still the most popular choice in engagement rings. The head secures the diamond. Prongs allow the diamond to catch the most light. A four-prong setting shows more of the diamond, but a six-prong setting is often more secure.*

- **Side Stone:** *Diamonds or other gemstones flank the main stone for additional sparkle or color. Popular side stone settings include "channel," which protects stones by keeping them flush and "bar-channel," which allows more light to enter the side stones.*

- **Three Stone:** *One diamond for the past, one for the present, and one for the future. Typically, the center diamond is larger than the two side stones.*

- **Pave (pah-vey):** *The main stone is surrounded by tiny diamonds to add sparkle and the illusion of greater size.*

As to actual setting design, consider your lifestyle and how well a certain setting will fit into it. If you're more active or outdoorsy, look for lower profile, less ornate, more sturdy choices, which are less likely to get knocked or caught on things. If she's more of a glamour woman, look for statement settings, with a higher stone profile and more intricate ring detailing or unique motif.

How to Buy a Diamond

Selecting Your Diamond

Throughout history, the diamond has been an enduring symbol of the powerful bond of love. Its strength, brilliance and value are as unique as the individuals who wear them. However, there are other considerations as well when buying a diamond. I have gathered some information to help educate you and help you understand the terminology and special considerations you need to make when selecting your perfect diamond prior to making a purchase and meeting with a jeweler.

Things You Need to Know

Your Preference and Your Budget

Combination of the elements of the 4 Cs, (as well as certification) is up to you.

Questions

- *Is clarity more important than* carat?
- *Is carat more important than color?*

Only you can decide what combination makes up the perfect choice for your diamond, jewelry, selecting an engagement ring.

About the 4 Cs

A diamond's worth is evaluated on four levels. We call these criteria the 4 Cs—carat, clarity, color, and cut.

Carat

Carat weight is the standard measure of a diamond's weight. The larger the diamond, the more rare it is. A carat (equivalent to 200 milligrams) consists of 100 points. Therefore a diamond of 75 points weighs 75 carats. It is important to remember that two diamonds of equal carat weight may have dramatically different values, depending upon the stone's cut, clarity, and color.

Clarity

Most diamonds contain very tiny natural characteristics called "inclusions." The size, number, position, nature, and color of these inclusions (as seen by the trained eye using ten-power magnification) will determine a stone's clarity grade. The smaller and less frequent the inclusions and surface blemishes, the more valuable and rare the gemstone.

Color

In nature, diamonds are found with a wide array of color—from colorless, to faint yellow or even brown, to rare pinks, blues, greens, and other colors known as "fancies." Selecting a diamond color is a matter of preference. Fancy yellow and pink diamonds make a creative and individual statement for an engagement ring. Most diamonds have at least a trace of yellow, brown, or grey body color. In general, the more colorless a diamond, the greater it's relative value. Diamonds that are graded D, E, and F are considered colorless. Diamonds graded G, H, and I are considered near-colorless. The color of your diamond will be reflected on your certificate.

Cut

How a diamond is cut is extremely important. In fact, it might be the most significant factor of the 4 Cs. The cut determines the diamond's reflective qualities and directly influences its value. A diamond's cut affects its brilliance. The better the cut, the brighter the diamond appears. How light enters a diamond, when a diamond is well cut, light enters through the table, travels to the pavilion and reflects from side to side, then pours out so the eye can see its fiery brilliance. Poorly cut diamonds have less fire and brilliance, because light enters through the table, hits the facets, and is ultimately lost out of the diamond's sides. A diamond's cut is sometimes confused with its shape. Shape is the actual appearance of a diamond, like round, pear, princess, oval and emerald etc.

How to Care for your Diamond

Many people think diamonds are indestructible, but they do require care. Diamonds are natural grease attractors. Wash your diamond regularly with jewelry cleaner and dry it with a lint-free cloth. For a diamond that is worn daily, this should be done once per week. Use brushes sparingly as they can damage the mounting. Chlorine can pit and dissolve gold alloys in your mounting. Do not wear your ring swimming in a pool or working with chlorine solutions. I recommend that you bring your diamond to your trusted jeweler for a periodic inspection and professional cleaning. This service sometimes can be free where you purchased your diamond engagement ring.

Diamond Certification

One of the more important steps in choosing a diamond is reviewing the diamond certificate, referred to in diamond grading labs as a grading report. This report documents the characteristics of a diamond, including the 4 Cs. Before purchasing a diamond, review a copy of its grading report as this is your guarantee of quality for that diamond.

Other Fine Jewelry

- *Amethyst Jewelry*
- *Aquamarine Jewelry*
- *Citrine Jewelry*
- *CZ Jewelry*
- *CZ Rings*
- *Diamond Jewelry*
- *Emerald Jewelry*
- *Garnet Jewelry*
- *Gold Jewelry*
- *Pearl Jewelry*
- *Platinum Jewelry*
- *Quartz Jewelry*
- *Ruby Jewelry*
- *Sapphire Jewelry*
- *Topaz Jewelry*
- *Turquoise Jewelry*

Best Jewelry Designers

- *Harry Winston*
- *Cartier*
- *Costis*
- *Van Cleff & Arpels*
- *Bvlgari*
- *Faraone Mennella*

- *Sicis Jewels*
- *Autore*
- *Efva Attling Stckholm*
- *Todd Reed*
- *Scott Kay*
- *Lydia Courteille*
- *Chopard*
- *Lugano Diamonds*
- *Gintare*

Best Luxury Watches

- *Jaeger – Lecoultre*
- *Richard Mille*
- *Vacheron*
- *Breguet*
- *Audemars Oiguet*
- *Patek Philippe*
- *Panerai*
- *Alange & Sohne*
- *Tag Heuer*
- *Urweerk*
- *Zenith*

Your Personal Study Guide Notes:

_____

_____

_____

_____

_____

_____

_____

_____

_____

_____

_____

_____

_____

_____

_____

_____

_____

_____

_____

_____

_____

_____

_____

_____

20

Passion for Shopping

Best Shopping Memories with My Mother

SHOPPING FOR DAYS with our classy mom, the great times growing up in a large family. So many off the chart memories with her and my father. Both parents were stylish, if I must say so. At an early age, we could shop from sun up to sun down.

We would go shopping for days at a time, looking for any and every fashionable, classy style of clothing, hats, gloves, handbags, designer shoes, and more shoes. Her favorite shoes were Salvatore Ferragamo. She dressed extremely well. Her fabulous accessories and classy clothes looked great on her and fit her body so well. My mother's style may have been a lovely classic dress, a blazer and skirt, her Armani business suits, gloves in the winter, mink coat, cashmere sweater set. She loved color. Her shoes were all so nice, heels and her one significant piece of fine jewelry and her great necklace to really make her outfit complete.

It's a lifestyle that I learned and came to love. She was well polished and classy. Great times! My passion for fashion came from my mom. Beautiful and great memories of my mother, as I sit at my desk in my custom Louis Vuitton desk chair, writing this very book you are reading, going down memory lane, thinking about the laughter, fine dining, the quality time we spent together as mother and daughter. Our time spent cannot be replaced, I'm grateful for the time and memories we had together.

Wow, how time flies. Way too much fun, shopping for trendy vintage apparel, visiting ultra-stylish boutiques it seems like all over the world. We started with breakfast in Beverly Hills, shopping on Rodeo Drive, enjoying the California sun, lunch at Neiman Marcus, dinner at the Ivy, and back to shopping at Saks Fifth Avenue. Oh my fabulous mother. Fashion was an early fix for me. My mother supported my love for fashion and glamour. I had a chance to learn from one of the best teachers ever. She taught me firsthand about fashion, style, image, poise and polishing, how to be a classy lady, my mother the best teacher ever, Mrs. Loretta Frink. Oh how I miss you.

I love giving back and helping women to connect with dressing for success, mirroring her true "it" factor for over thirty years. I have shared what I've learned about fashion and style with women and single moms. To me this is rewarding and it feels good. I love being a different, fabulous, caring, God fearing, and independent thinking woman. I don't think I will ever change who I am. Coco Chanel she said it best, "In order to be irreplaceable, one must always be different."

Find Your Fabulous Apparel and Accessories

You do not need to have the best fashion sense, biggest closet, or deepest pockets to create a credible professional image. You do not need to look like a factory manufactured professional either. Remember, your image is not just about your clothing, but is a reflection of your total persona. Your individuality communicates self-confidence, creativity and leadership. The key is to project your uniqueness while maintaining the appropriateness for your profession and you will build the credibility you need to succeed.

Best Accessories

Eye-catching and statement-making extras that would make any discerning accessory lover rejoice! The accessories you'll be shopping and lusting to get your hands on come the new season and you can guarantee these trimmings will inevitably land on the wish list of every "it" woman around. Feast your eyes on the best accessories on the runways by way of standout shoes, covetable bags, distinctive Sunnis, bold bijoux, and all the extras spotted that add up to a major fashion moment, both on and off the catwalk. Start prepping your shopping guide.

Earrings have gained popularity for both sexes in recent years, but they really are only appropriate for females in the career fair/interviewing arena. Wear one pair of simple earrings for these events. Watches are good for both sexes, same caliber as the rest of your appearance. Rings and bracelets can be worn but in moderation and if they are essential to you. One ring is most appropriate. Jewelry should never be a distraction for you or the employer. Shoes should be pumps or medium heels. Purses should be medium-or-small-sized purse that matches your outfit.

- *Classy Accessories: Classy accessories, wearing a single ring, a pair of small earrings, and a small necklace is fine. Wearing a suit with a ring on every finger, watch, bracelet, an elaborate clip, a belt, a scarf around the neck is not. A soft and gentle looking accessory, small to medium in size, is the feminine choice. Delicate and antique looking with curved designs adds to the wispy ideal that is all female. They often like to wear accessories and scarves, matte to semi-sheen in different colors. The feminine woman loves her pearls.*

- **Classic Accessories:** *Classic accessories, are simple, small to medium in size, and nothing too extreme in fashion. The classic consists of good quality and is current, accessories, classic in style, and are always coordinated with the entire look. There are no more than two to three colors in the entire look with stockings to complement the fabulous look.*

- **Elegant Accessories:** *Elegant accessories, are real jewelry with gemstones and pearls or the best quality in faux jewelry, but nothing too glittery. This woman loves to accessorize with scarves. The hosiery is chosen with natural colors and is very sheer to blend with the outfit or the shoes they are wearing. The heels are in a medium size.*

- **Dramatic Accessories:** *Dramatic accessories, are drawn to the unusual in both look and feel, preferring large scale, unique, and individual designs. The flare is to be one of a kind, striking and distinctive.*

- **Feminine Accessories:** *Feminine accessories, are soft and gentle looking accessories, small to medium in size, is the feminine choice. Delicate, antique looking with curved designs adds to the wispy ideal that is all female. They often like to wear accessories and scarves, matte to semi-sheen in different colors. The feminine woman loves her pearls.*

- **Sporty Accessories:** *Sporty accessories, are minimal and simple. Like classic women, they do not like too much of it, they like their comfort. Simple accessories are plenty for them as they prefer relaxed handbags with sporty watches and accessories. Shoe styles for this woman are medium to low heels.*

- **Sexy Accessories:** *Sexy accessories, are shiny gold or any sparkly jewelry. They often wear multiple bracelets or rings. Strappy shoes in high or flat heels, earrings in any form, drop hoops, medium in size, often complement the sexy outfit.*

Make Accessories Work on a Budget

Whether they are shoes, sunglasses, earrings, bracelets, necklaces, belts, scarves, or handbags, find the ones that you love best and buy many at low-cost shops. The key is to dress up a wardrobe many different ways without blowing your budget. The best thing to do is buy all sorts of accessories for as little as you can. These keep your wardrobe interesting by adding color, texture, shape and bling! Find the best inexpensive looking jewelry, trendy shoes, and hair clips. Color pumps to pump up your black suit for work or jeans and a t-shirt. Hollywood stars use the same tricks, just on a different budget. Nobody knows what to look at first! When you get ready to leave the house, look into a full-length mirror with your entire outfit, including a hat or handbag if included. Mirror daily the fabulous look you desire.

"Elegance does not consist in putting on a new dress."

— Coco Chanel

Your Personal Study Guide Notes:

_____

_____

_____

_____

_____

_____

_____

_____

_____

_____

_____

_____

_____

_____

_____

_____

_____

_____

_____

_____

_____

_____

_____

_____

_____

_____

Paris Shopper's Paradise

Planning a shopping trip and tour gives you insider access, exclusive store discounts, and an exciting and relaxing way to experience Paris. Discover Paris in the style you prefer! Both walking tours and tours by car are available, with stops along the way at sights of interest of your choice for photo opportunities! The tours are ideal for those who want to shop and sight see, exploring fascinating neighborhoods and unique boutiques.

Find Your Fabulous Designer Deals

Don't be afraid to shop in thrift stores and outlet malls. I can't tell you how many things I've been able to snag. The key is to go into an area that is more well-to-do or exclusive for thrift store shopping. Often people with a lot of money can discard things faster for new items such as great sweaters, blazers, handbags, you name it! My last purchase there was actually a set of hot rollers that retailed at $70 that I picked up for $16! I bought an $80 pair of designer shoes that were never worn for $26! I'll admit, you have to make some time to sift through a lot of duds till you find a few keepers, but it is well worth it. Buy items that have their original bold color, no fading! Make sure there are no holes or stains. If there is a small area that is inconspicuous and the item is a steal, by all means grab the item if you can fix it. You can also find some fun handbags, belts and jewelry there too! Who doesn't love a deal? So whether you want to get a jump start on holiday shopping or just love to shop like me, I've pulled the best designer outlet malls and recommended nearby places to stay.

Five Outlet Malls worth Visiting

- **Chicago Premium Outlets**
  1650 Premium Outlets Boulevard
  Aurora, IL
  (630) 585-2200

premiumoutlets.com/Chicago
The Draw: Michael Kors, Juicy Couture, and Diesel are just a few of the brands that savvy visitors can score for way less than their original prices at the 120 outlet stores in this center, located forty-five minutes west of the Windy City. Bonus: Check the website for hotel discounts too.

- **Desert Hills Premium Outlets**
  48400 Seminole Drive
  Cabazon, CA
  (951) 849-6641
  premiumoutlets.com/desert hills
  The Draw: Surrounded by mountains, practically a coconut's throw from the famed Palm Springs Resort, this center is a West Coast mainstay. Inside, shoppers snag reduced-price finds from Jimmy Choo, Diane von Furstenberg, and other top designer labels.

- **Houston Premium Outlets**
  29300 Hempstead Road
  Cypress, TX
  (281) 304-5820
  premiumoutlets.com/Houston
  The Draw: This newbie on the outlet scene keeps shoppers happy with stores like Nine West, Elie Tahari, and Ann Taylor Factory under its bustling roof. For even more savings, join the VIP Shopper Club on the website for exclusive coupons and updates.

- **Las Vegas Premium Outlets**
  875 South Grand Central Parkway
  Las Vegas, NV
  (702) 474-7500
  premiumoutlets.com/Las Vegas
  The Draw: Just five minutes off the Strip, this is one of the largest outlet centers in the US. Among the 150 stores, you'll

find Polo Ralph Lauren, True Religion, and Lacoste—all good spots to blow your casino winnings.

- **North Georgia Premium Outlets**
  800 Highway 400 South
  Dawsonville, GA
  (706) 216-3609
  premiumoutlets.com/North Georgia
  The Draw: A quaint Georgian village setting greets visitors shopping for Calvin Klein, Pottery Barn, Cole Haan, and more than 130 others at this hot spot, located just forty-five minutes north of Atlanta.

- **Philadelphia Premium Outlets**
  18 West Light cap Road
  Limerick, PA
  (610) 495-9000
  premiumoutlets.com/Philadelphia
  The Draw: Take a break from all of those Philly cheesesteaks and head over to this recently expanded outlet center. It's loaded with stores like French Connection, Puma, and Neiman Marcus Last Call, so you're sure to burn off the calories.

- **Seattle Premium Outlets**
  10600 Quil Ceda Boulevard
  Tulalip, WA
  (360) 654-3000
  premiumoutlets.com/Seattle
  The Draw: Hit up this outlet mall where Kenneth Cole, Restoration Hardware, J.Crew, and other stores offer their merchandise at prices that'll make you forget about that Seattle rain.

- **Waikele Premium Outlets**
  94-790 Lumiaina Street
  Waipahu, HI
  (808) 676-5656

premiumoutlets.com/waikele
The Draw: Say aloha to outlet shopping in Hawaii at a mall well worth a mini hiatus from the beach. You'll find LeSportsac, MaxMara, Coach, and other stores that will leave you with enough cash to buy a round of Mai Tais later.

- **Woodbury Common Premium Outlets**
  498 Red Apple Court
  Central Valley, NY
  (845) 928-4000
  premiumoutlets.com/Woodbury Common
  The Draw: This outlet giant, home to 220 stores, has earned legendary status among city-dwelling Fashionista who want high fashion on the cheap. An hour north of NYC, it features Betsey Johnson, Chanel, M Missoni, Swarovski, and Theory.

- **Wrentham Village Premium Outlets**
  One Premium Outlets Boulevard
  Wrentham, MA
  (508) 384-0600
  premiumoutlets.com/Wrentham
  The Draw: After drooling over full-priced items along Boston's Newbury Street, make the quick trip (just thirty-five minutes south of the city) to one of the 170 stores at this retail center. At Kate Spade, Saks Fifth Avenue Off 5th, Salvatore Ferragamo, or Banana Republic, you'll find similar (if not the exact same) goods at half the price.

World's Top Outlet Stores Around the Globe

- *Maine*
- *Japan*
- *New York*
- *Milan*
- *Swiss Mendrisio*

- *England*
- *France*
- *Italy*

New York–based stylist Ellianna Placas is an A-list fashionista who's dressed celebrities from Oprah Winfrey to Brazilian super-model Camila Alves. Yet when she travels say, to Milan Fashion Week, she always reserves a few days to scour outlet malls. She'll even cross the Swiss border to the Fox Town outlet store in Mendrisio. Why? "It's Prada, Prada, Prada," she swoons, "and everything else you can think of at more than half off!" Placas isn't alone, of course: the lure of the discount calls all types of shoppers. Outlets exist all over the globe, from Maine to Japan and the best ones are destinations in and of themselves. For the bargain hunter, unearthing a deal on Gucci, Pucci, or Dolce & Gabbana can be just as adrenaline pumping as visiting the *Mona Lisa*.

So where and how did they begin? The late Dexter Shoe magnate Harold Alfond is credited with inventing the outlet concept in the 1960s at his factory in Maine, instead of junking imperfect pairs, he'd sell them at a reduced price. Since then, outlets have become a major worldwide business: They're the ideal way of off-loading (often imperceptibly) imperfect merchandise as well as past-season premium goodies at deep discounts, often with no discernible difference in quality from what's sold at your local department store (albeit in season).

As outlets took off around the globe, they underwent some adaptations too. Some are brand-specific, like the one for Le Creuset, the high-end cookware company based in the tiny northern French town of Fresnoy-le-Grand. Brits come here by the boatload to snap up cast-iron cooking pots and pans for around 50 percent off. Other outlets cram tons of designer brands into a one-stop shopping experience. More than two hundred stores make up Woodbury Common Premium Outlets, for example, ninety minutes north of New York City. So while the luxe shops of Fifth Avenue are great for window-shopping, head to Woodbury to buy. After all, you'll find some of the same brands, Burberry, Armani, Coach, as you will in the city, but up to 65 percent off.

Treat malls like these as you would a destination: Pick up a map and get to know its geography. "Outlets are set up for optimal shopping efficiency," says Danica Lo, the editor of Racked. com. "Woodbury Common is shaped like a flower, so start from the middle and go around each petal."

Then, hit the most important place first. Brands with lots of outlets (like Nike or Banana Republic) don't have great deals, but designers with just a few stores, like Gucci and Anya Hindmarch, will usually offer steeper slashes.

Bicester Village, England

Come to the town of Oxfordshire for cool Britannia at a cut price, up to 70 percent off. Expect leather goods from Smythson (its creative director is Brit first-lady-in-waiting Samantha Cameron) as well as classic separates from Jaeger and heirloom knits by Pringle of Scotland. Recent additions: Purses from Anya Hindmarch and avant-garde unmentionables from Agent Provocateur.

Insider Tip: There's a free three-hour personal shopping assistance program offered on weekday mornings and afternoons. Book ahead atstyleconsultancy@bicestervillage.com

L.L. Bean, Freeport

Look for the giant signature boot out front to locate this monolithic bargain bin amid the raft of high-end outlet stores on Freeport's Main Street. L.L. Bean's practical, hunter-chic (albeit not high fashion) clothing is up to 60 percent off at its factory store. And in case the urge for bargains keeps anyone awake at night, its open 24/7, 365 days a year.

Insider Tip: Don't miss the second floor, where plaid housewares and furniture with the L.L. Bean label are also deeply discounted.

Gotemba Premium Outlets, Japan

The largest outlet mall in Japan, just sixty miles west of Tokyo in Shizuoka, is pilgrimage-worthy for two reasons. First, its two-hundred-strong shop selection includes rarities like Maison Martin Margiela, Balenciaga, and Bottega Veneta at 25 to 65 percent off retail. Second, the views of Mount Fuji are spectacular.

Insider Tip: The larger, Western-friendly sizes are remaindered more readily here and these racks are full of handy Ls and XLs.

Fox Town Factory Store, Switzerland

Switzerland may be famed for swanky banking, swoony chocolates, and self-winding watches, but thanks to Fox Town, in the town of Mendrisio, it's owed kudos for style too. This outlet mall is crammed with local labels, like underwear icon Hanro, at 50 to 80 percent off. But since Milan is just across the border, it's only forty-five minutes away by train or car, there's also a slew of Italian marques, including Missoni, Dolce & Gabbana, and chic sneaker maker Superga.

Insider Tip: If you're making a day jaunt from Italy, remember to pack your passport. Not only will you be passing in and out of the EU via Swiss immigration, but you'll need it to reclaim tax on purchases for export.

Space, Italy

Everything about this Tuscan outlet is designed to obscure its true purpose as the best place in the world to find Miuccia Prada's gems off-price. There's the obscure name, plus the impossible-to-find location. Space sits in the middle of a gloomy, gray industrial park close to Florence. Once inside, grab a ticket like you would in an old-school grocery and wait for the chance to shop last season's styles at up to 50 percent off retail.

Insider Tip: Again, Space is not the easiest of outlets to find. Follow signs for I Pellettieri d'Italia or tell the GPS "Via Levanella."

Woodbury Common Premium Outlets, New York

Less than ninety minutes from Manhattan's Fifth Avenue, savvy shoppers can find the same branded merchandise at up to 65 percent off, thanks to this 220-strong ultra-luxe outlet hub. Skip the Gap and Banana Republic that are in every off-price mall and linger instead at luxe rarities like Gucci, Pucci, and Christian Dior.

Insider Tip: From Manhattan, hop the express bus service from Port Authority in Midtown ($42 round trip, www.grayline.com).

Wedgwood & Royal Doulton Outlet, England

Here you'll find cut-rate prices on cut glass, like 30 percent off a raft of blue-chip British tabletop brands like Waterford crystal. This must-stop is a combined outlet store on the campus of china icon Wedgwood, in Stoke-on-Trent, the heart of Britain's pottery-producing district. Also on sale: Royal Doulton and Edinburgh Crystal, mostly end-of-line or discontinued styles so stock up.

Insider Tip: The most outrageous bargains (up to 75 percent off retail) are on the imperfect china, though most of it is has defects barely visible to the casual eye.

Le Creuset Outlet, France

Follow the hordes of fresh-off-the-boat Brits as they stampede into this small farmhouse-like store just outside of Calais. Sure, there are Le Creuset outlets in malls across America, but this is the mother lode for high-end cast-iron cooking pots and pans for around 50 percent off.

Insider Tip: Send an email to serviceconso@lecreuset.fr in advance and the helpful staff will check stock levels to see if the item that you're yearning for is available at a discount.

The Mall, Tuscany and Italy

Imagine Palm Beach's Worth Avenue transplanted to a Tuscan hillside with prices slashed up to 70 percent. None of the stores here are a makeweight—there are standalone from each of the Gucci group labels like Bottega Veneta, Balenciaga, and Stella McCartney, as well as Zegna, Armani, Fendi, and Loro Piana. Crucially, even though this is largely last season's stock, it isn't limited to the coutré.

Insider Tip: From Maine to Japan, these discount outlets are worth traveling for. If you are looking to score a fabulous deal.

Remember also, beware the companies whose outlets stock merchandise produced specifically for them. Those aren't discount deals, just cheap stuff. "It mostly happens with the mass market, but the labels are different from the normal store," Lo explains. "The colors are often reversed; the Gap has a different label all together."

Related Links

- *50 Best Fashion Stores in America*
- *10 International Outlets Worth the Trek*
- *40 Best Online Shopping Sites*
- *Expert Online Shopping Tips*
- *Vintage Shopping 101*
- *6 Transitional Outfits to Ease into Spring*

Your Personal Study Guide Notes:

_____

_____

_____

_____

_____

_____

_____

_____

_____

_____

_____

_____

_____

_____

_____

_____

_____

_____

_____

_____

_____

_____

_____

_____

21

I Understand Why

THIRTY YEARS LATER, I understand why I was created to
give. A lot of my fear came from the unknown. You may not realize it, but until you learn how to overcome your fears and know
that fear may have created a stronghold in your mind, you will
not be able to move forward. Here's an example of how to overcome it. I had a lot of fear of the unknown and ran from my best
life. I had a great career. I was placed in the top ten of executives
in high demand and I knew that. It still wasn't clear why I lived
in such fear until one day, I asked God for a clear path to help me
be stronger in my walk. He said, "Have no fear I'm with you." He
started tearing down the walls of the unknown. He showed me
where I had built a wall over the years. The wall was too high even
for me to climb. I'm sharing with you what I discovered during
my quest to seek a better understanding and when I asked him

to clear my path and to do his will, I also asked him to guide me and to give me wisdom and he did.

Over Thirty Years

Thirty years of teaching dressing for success, coaching, training, styling women, and working closely with fashion designers, makeup artists, and photographers, some of the best at their craft throughout my professional career, I can't tell you how many times I wanted to give up my passion for fashion and style. Yes, on many occasions I've literally wanted to throw in the towel, I just wanted out and to do something different. The moment I thought I was moving to do other cool things, my manager called with another project.

Ask for Forgiveness

I have experienced some amazing things while writing this guide book. I've let go of all the things that I cannot change, things that are not God like, I asked for forgiveness from others and released them from my unforgiving hold. When you release all that poison and distraction, you find peace within and it's amazing. I asked God to please forgive me for allowing poison, distraction, and these walls to be built so high. I almost prevented God's blessing and favor from pouring into my life. With God's power, the most amazing thing began to happen. My prayers were answered one by one; it happened so quickly. I tell you once you let go of the past and rid yourself of distractions and poison, he turns on the light. You can see clearly... it's on!

I didn't choose this career, it chose me. Now I know why. It was what I needed professionally and personally. People ask how I keep up my look and style; it looks so fabulous, they say. Well, to all who ask: the little girl with a mind and heart for fashion, the women with the fierce attitude, and fabulous women, I'm committed to a clean, stress-free, healthy, and God-fearing life.

My Dream

I have always known there was more to life than this. What I really dream of... not just a fabulous lifestyle. I dream of fabulous, beautiful, confident moms and daughters spending quality time together, laughing a lot, going to the beach, playing dress up, doing fun, creative things, taking lots of pictures together, displaying their photos throughout the home. You'd be surprised at the effect that visual art has. It adds value to your life for years to come. Keep in mind, money, or time should not stop you from spending as much time, and I mean quality time, with your daughter(s). Teach her how to pray and pray together. Read books together. Have a mom and daughter day. Do things a little girl enjoys. As a grown woman your daughter will mirror her mother, a role model, a mother, not her best friend, that will come when she has an idea of the true value of your role. Build great memories together, take lots of pictures, be kind, let her know you love her and she will return the love for many years to come.

Mothers, teach your daughter by example. Hold a good life, as one of your highest standards, value and build a bond with your daughter. I pray that you all have a strong desire for love, strong bond, clear vision, and be a role model for young ladies across the globe. This is my dream, prayer, and wish for women and daughters to pass it on to others so their lives, hearts, minds, bodies, and souls can be blessed. This is a movement for change in mother-and-daughter relationships. There is nothing like a mother and daughter love.

The growth that I've experienced over the past fifty-three years has been incredible. As I reflect on the love I have for the growth and development of well-rounded women, I feel like I have learned more and have had more relevant growth and more focused conversations in the past three months than at any point in my career. I want to share and empower women on how to grow.

"People that value its privileges above its principles
soon lose both."

— Dwight D. Eisenhower

Values are the principles that influence and guide your behavior. Keep in mind, when and where they're absent, self-interest reigns supreme. People begin to protect their own turf, putting their own power and privileges ahead of the well-being of the people. So practice best principles and guide your behavior a team's values are vulnerable to time, turnover and growth.

Value Threats

Leaders have to counteract each of these threats with a specific strategy in order to make sure their team's values stay strong. Just remember there are people who are in worse situations. Try not to complain about anything that you can work on. Instead, take actions to improve each situation as it pops up. Overcome bad situations in life. When something is not going the way you planned, don't worry or throw away your goals, because at some point, everyone has to succeed in, over, around, or through rough spots. Life wouldn't seem bright without loads of dark drama. There is no one in this world who lives a life without shadows and problems.

After being an executive and providing training, I'm able to clearly realize my life's purpose, my vision. Most importantly, I felt confident and worthy to take the time and necessary steps to make it come to fruition. I thank him for giving me the ability, education, experience, the kind and pure heart to lead. Thank you, God for choosing me, never leaving my side, for trusting and believing in me. I love you for all that you do.

Your Personal Study Guide Notes:

_____

_____

_____

_____

_____

_____

_____

_____

_____

_____

_____

_____

_____

_____

_____

_____

_____

_____

_____

_____

_____

_____

_____

_____

22

What Is the Importance of the Author?

WHAT I HOPE to contribute with this book is full self-compassion for all women, moms, and daughters, to be fabulous and embrace who you are, love yourself like your favorite dress!

Family and friends who know me as I am understand where I have been and they accept what I have become and still gently allow me to grow.

You see, for the past thirty years, I've been blessed to have just that and more, to dress and mirror my own style. It's pretty fabulous. Growing up in a two-parent home, they made and gave the rules. We lived by my parents' rules. No doubt it's a lifestyle Dad instilled and taught to us on many levels. You did not and you could not get away with anything!

The little girl with big dreams carved out her custom master plan, so she thought. I once had a dream that I was going to Hollywood. In my dream I was making big time movies, movies about my family and movies about my teachers. Crazy. My dream has come true! I launched Lauren Fabulous Firm, LLC in 2012. I am the founder and CEO of my firm, business leader, entrepreneur, style icon, and now the author of this book you are currently reading. In writing this book, I'm speaking of professional experiences and lifestyle(s). It's great how things work themselves out. My parents gave us a wonderful life to the best of their ability. They supported their thirteen children's dreams, education, exposure to world travel, encouraging and kind words, being strong, and keeping God first in our lives and obeying his word. Mom would say things like, "If you're not sure and you feel confused, stop, wait on your answer from God, I promise he will let you know when to go or when you need to make your next move." I share with you today because we all have a message and desire to share with the world. Keep in mind God knows your plan, now seek him for direction and guidance on what you were born to do on this earth. Feel free to use my mother's above direction that she gave to me; it has helped me and I still use it today in my daily life. I love my parents for their ability to guide me.

Let's talk. Who is Lauren Freeman? Humble but passionate in my creative endeavors to play my role as one of the next global media business leaders, style icons, authors, and philanthropists, to accept and establish myself as a highly respected and admired public figure. I want to challenge you to know your value, fall in love with yourself; know your look and embrace your fabulous lifestyle. I believe every woman should first capture the attention of self. Fall in love again with self, figure out which color looks best on your complexion. Recommit to self-confidence, be creative, have fun, be passionate about your journey. This is a movement to heal, to bring joy to your soul, and to celebrate a healthy and more fabulous you! Join our movement at www.laurenfabulousfirm.com

Practicing and Developing Better Listening Skills

Now a grown woman, what I learned as a little girl still makes sense. I can still hear my parents saying, "Lauren, do you have your listening ears on?" Listening skills and the ability to really hear, I believe this comes with lots of practice. With focused and persistent parents, it has made me a better listener. I'm glad they stayed persistent. It afforded me the know-how and the ability to listen, to learn, and not listen to talk. I know when to stop and wait for a clear answer and focus on the task at hand. Oh yes, I still practice listening as an adult.

Growing Pains

From the pain, through the changes, until now, I'm a pro at waiting for the green light; however, those growing pains bring tears, heartache, sleepless nights and it seems like endless nightmares. It can break up a family and sometimes just loss of family bonding time. Do you realize how many times you will stumble and fall? I've stumbled so many times, until God blessed me to stumble myself to a vertical position. Now I know how it works. I'm living proof. His love for you and his guidance is always there. He heals the broken heart. He can work it out. Once you give your heart to him, give it all or it can take a lifetime, it's up to you. When you decide to give God your all and follow your best life, he can heal you and he will set you free. Live your fabulous lifestyle.

My Life Experiences

Yes, my life experiences have made it easy to be Lauren Freeman. I'm free because I know Jesus Christ. He made me, he knows my heart. I have a pure, kind, and clean heart. My mind, my body, my spirit, and my soul are right. I'm no longer afraid to share my life's journey. When life doesn't make sense, I have come to a point where I'm no longer afraid of the unknown. I know what it is that I must do! I have high standards, values, integrity, and my respect for self, and others are in line. I expect excellence and I choose to mirror an excellent, fabulous lifestyle. I'm a loving daughter, mother, wife, grandmother, sister, sister's keeper, best friend, fashionista, style icon, entrepreneur, and author.

My Son Ray

Ray, my firstborn. Ray, from birth, you have been the driving force and my motivation in every aspect growing up together. As a single parent growing up just the two of us was such a special time. Words cannot express my gratitude for that time in our lives; it's one of the reasons I am so passionate about our relationship. We are a true testament of how a mother and son should be. A mother's love for her son and a son's love for his mother. I cherish our memories together. I love to see you smile, the joy you bring, your passion for life, and your focus to work hard to be the best at whatever you do. Ray, you are abundantly blessed and well loved. Thank you for the unforgettable memories. My time invested in you is valuable and I truly appreciate you for believing in God, yourself, and our mother-and-son relationship. Through our obstacles and our own personal growth, we have made it. It seems so long ago, but when I look at you now, I see so much of me in you. I see your heart's desire, your love for God and family. It is hard to figure out all that goes into making a great son. You are a great husband to Jasmine, father and a role model for your son and daughter. Thadus Ray III and Logan Nicole, you all are my angels... What a blessing, Ray you are a son who can be mirrored; I am honored to be your mother and you are the precious legacy we leave. I'm proud to know you are well designed and are built to teach by example and pass it on! I love you so much. I love you like our pearly white teeth. What a joy to have you all in my life!

My Daughter Hasani

On March 4, 1994, at 7:45 am, in Beverly Hills, California, on my thirty-third birthday, a little princess was born. Wow, who could ask for a better gift; my little perfect angel. I knew from birth that our mother-and-daughter love would be built on trust and open communication. We would spend many days in Beverly Hills shopping and dining. I spent lots of time on the beach, traveling, and having a fabulous good time with my little girl. We did beauty pageants, took home way too many awards. I remember the last pageant she had won so many trophies and awards we needed help taking them off the stage. We had fun playing dress up. Just like your Mom may have told you when you were growing up, you have to have a mind of your own. Thank you for allowing that to develop and never change. I love you for that, and thank you for understanding all the not-so-good times, when I knew what was best for you. Growing up together, two strong-minded women finding their way through their passion and love for the arts. It seems like yesterday receiving a special card designed by Hasani. The passion for art, special gifts designed by you, special pictures, and the cute cards, especially the cards when you did something wrong (I knew by the design of the card) and, yes, let's not forget your coordinated fashion shows with your friends, the crazy photos, and too many great times to list. Oh, how I cherish those memories.

Writing this reminded me of your thirteenth birthday. You would always write us a wish list and you would tape it to our bedroom door. The thirteenth birthday was different because it was spent in New York on Broadway, the birth to your first music, dance, more art classes, and sewing workshops. Oh, how could I forget your Beatles phase, shopping all over the world for books and photos of the Beatles. You even designed a mural of the Beatles at your school. Fashion, sketching and drawing books were your thing. How could I forget your first piano concert?

So many fabulous memories. Hasani, you are very beautiful to me, brilliant and intelligent. You have a pure, impeccable taste in fashion, you are super talented and a true star child and young lady. I'm elated and thankful we can have a mom and daughter open communication between us. Thank you for this, after turning twenty years of age, I believe you see the value and understand the role of old parents (This is how kids look at their parents). We just seem old. Your parents can be the most important people in your life. Even if you don't always get along with them, be kind to them and always respect them. Just remember, without them, you wouldn't be here.

Although they are not able to fulfill your wants and dreams, they are still your parents. Value your virtues. You are intelligent and you are a gift from God. You are blessed to have great skills and talent, such as fashion, style, design, sewing, drawing and playing the piano. I see how you practice. Keep focused, work hard and smart, and do your best. However, being a classy young lady, know your style, know who you are and know your purpose in life. Have fun. Keep God first, value your family, respect yourself, be excellent at everything you do. These will open doors, Hasani. Whatever you do, it's important to be happy. Get your education and do what you love for a career. I have shared this message with my kids as a child to adulthood. Let people see how good you are by exposing your work and talent, stay humble, think excellent, and be excellent in everything you do! The world is yours for as long as I can give it to you. Hasani, I love you like shopping in Paris.

Lauren's Fabulous Style

I have been told that no one represents your style better than your own unique beauty and personality. I want other women to validate their style from the selections in Chapter 12, Who Are You, as a way for all of us to learn. Most of all, I want these decisions to ignite and inspire conversations in your social settings about how they might apply their own style, journey and lifestyle. Then share your thoughts on who you are from chapter 12. Who Are You, helped you to identify your unique beauty, personality and style. I invite you to visit www.laurenfabulousfirm.com to continue sharing who you are and your fabulous choice of style with the rest of the world.

I want to share my personal style and look with you. My style is classy with an elegant look, a style that reflects my own individual personality. My choice of style is simple, classy with somewhat of a custom, personal twist, and fashion forward must-have accessories. The key to mastering your own personal style is to have the confidence to carry yourself with grace and poise. It is important that you understand the how, when and what of the fashion rules (Write your fabulous style in your personal study guide notes below). My hope is for you to embrace your style; have a lasting transformation; shake up your makeup; search for inspiring ideas that make your life richer and set goals in your guide. It's no secret that it's time to throw out your old beauty routine and jump start your makeover. Follow the thirteen step makeover, have fun while mirroring your new fabulous style made easy! Be grateful for everything you have. Love life and stay fabulous!

"A girl should be two things, Classy and Fabulous."

— Coco Chanel

Your Personal Study Guide Notes:

_____

_____

_____

_____

_____

_____

_____

_____

_____

_____

_____

_____

_____

_____

_____

_____

_____

_____

_____

_____

_____

_____

_____

Author Picks

- *Coco Chanel*
- *Yves Saint Laurent*
- *Christian Louboutin*
- *Christian Dior*
- *Jean Paul Guiltier*
- *Christian Lacroix*
- *Tom Ford*
- *Louis Vuitton*
- *Ralph Lauren*
- *Gucci*
- *Donatella Versace*
- *Giorgio Armani*

Best Fashion Designers

- *Tom Ford*
- *Karl Lagerfeld*
- *Zac Posen*
- *Stefano and Somenico*
- *Alexander McQueen*
- *Coco Chanel*
- *Phoebe Philo*
- *Valentino*
- *Diane Von Furstenberg*
- *Giorgio Armani*

- *Stella McCartney*
- *Oscar De La Renta*
- *Marc Jacobs*
- *Riccardo Tisci*
- *Donatella Versace*

Best Women's Designer Shoes

- *Louis Vuitton*
- *Brian Atwood*
- *Stuart Weitzman*
- *Alexander McQueen*
- *Christian Louboutin*
- *Miu Miu*
- *Walter Steiger*
- *Manolo Blahnik*
- *Jimmy Choo*

Best Perfumes

- *Coco Chanel No. 5*
- *Creed*
- *Kilian*
- *Amouage*
- *Bond No. 9*
- *Clive Christian No. 1*
- *Lalique*
- *Puredistance 1*

Best Sexy Lingerie

- *Parah*
- *I.D. Sarrieri*
- *Intenzioni*
- *Agent Provocateur*
- *Eres*
- *Chamela*
- *Chantelle*
- *Bordelle*
- *Andres Sarda*
- *La Perla*
- *Fleur of England*
- *Guia La Bruna*

Your Personal Study Guide Notes:

_____

_____

_____

_____

_____

_____

_____

_____

_____

_____

_____

_____

_____

_____

_____

_____

_____

_____

_____

_____

_____

_____

_____

Fabulous Goals and Wishes List

For all of my fashion-forward fabulous fashionistas, you will want to create a goals and wishes list. Here is what to include:

Collect pictures to illustrate a sample basic wardrobe. A basic wardrobe should include a basic coat, suit with skirt, and pants, several coordinated jackets, tops, blouses or sweaters, basic dress or sleeveless sheath dress, basic outfit that could be worn for dress up or formal costume, basic rain coat, and sportswear.

Find clothing care articles and booklets to place in your study guide. Add tags you take off your new garments. Store them in your study guide with a description of the garment and the date of purchase. Now, you will have your cleaning and washing instructions handy. Find magazine or catalog pictures that express your personality type, compose a short paragraph telling yourself why you like those particular clothes.

Find pictures of different ideas for accessorizing your present wardrobe. Include pictures of accessories that are wrong for you and make a note why they are wrong. Add pictures of proper foundation garments for your figure's needs. Add a picture of a future foundation purchase. Devote one page to drawing and explaining your future plans for organizing your closet and drawers.

Find color illustrations of your colors and write a short essay on why they are right for you. Collect pictures of future basic wardrobe items which now include your line, style and color.

Collect samples of fabric and designs that are good for you. Look for samples that are appropriate year-round. Do a twice-a-year inventory and include pictures of your future wardrobe plans in your study guide.

Gather pictures of things you value and then decide how your values influence your clothing choices.

Select an image you would like to be identified with and list the types of garments you could wear to portray this image and the values it reflects.

258 | Lauren Freeman

Your Personal Study Guide Notes:

_____

_____

_____

_____

_____

_____

_____

_____

_____

_____

_____

_____

_____

_____

_____

_____

_____

_____

_____

_____

_____

_____

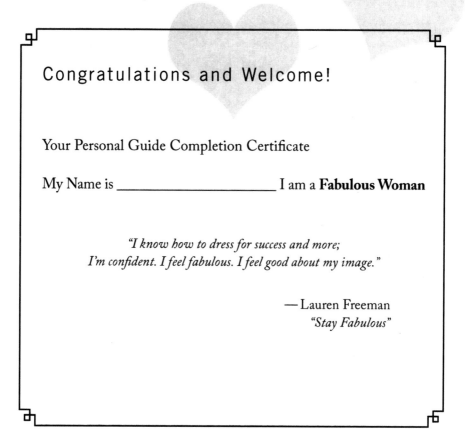

Congratulations and Welcome!

Your Personal Guide Completion Certificate

My Name is _____ I am a **Fabulous Woman**

"I know how to dress for success and more;
I'm confident. I feel fabulous. I feel good about my image."

— Lauren Freeman
"Stay Fabulous"

Support Groups for Women

Organizations

- *Women's Rights Charity / womenforwomen.org*
- *Womenforwomen.org Help a Woman Regain Dignity & Hope*
- *Start A Non-Profit Org—Form A Non-Profit Org In 3 Steps*
- *LegalZoom.com/Non-Profit*
- *Apply for Grants—Your grant money search stops here*
- *USAGrantApplications.org*
- *Apply For Free Grants / UnitedStatesGrants.Org*
- *www.UnitedStatesGrants.Org*
- *National Organization for Women (NOW)*
- *www.now.org*
- *Frisco Women League—Frisco, TX*
- *www.friscowomensleague.org*
- *Women Organized to Resist and Defend*
- *www.defendwomensrights.org*

- *MADRE / Demanding Rights, Resources & Results for Women*
- *www.madre.org*
- *Soroptimist: Women's Organization / Volunteer Opportunities*
- *www.soroptimist.org*
- *African American Women's Organization / National Council of Negro*
- *www.ncnw.org*
- *20 Women's Organizations You Need to Know / Diversity Best*
- *www.diversitybestpractices.com*

Related to Women's Organizations

- *Women's Organizations Mission Statements*
- *Women's Health Organizations*
- *Women's Business Organizations*
- *Arab Women's Organizations*
- *Women's Organizations for Rights and Development*
- *National Organizations for Women (NOW)*

Women's Shelters

- *Global Network of Women's Shelters (www.gnws.org/en/work/global-data-count.html)*
- *Global Network of Women's Shelters—History (www.gnws.org/en/about/history.html*
- *Global Network of Women's Shelters / Facebook (http://www.facebook.com/GlobalNetwork)*
- *Avon Foundation: Global Believe Fund (www.avonfoundation.org/causes/domestic/global-believe-fund)*

- *Domestic Violence–Domestic Abuse Shelter–A New Beginning (www.domesticabuse shelter.org/InfoDomesticViolence.htm)*

- *History of Battered Women's Movement / Saint Martha's Hall (saintmarthas.org/resources/history-of-battered-womens-movement)*

- *Homeless Statistics / Shelter 2.0 (www.shelter20.com/homeless-statistics)*

- *Women's Shelter Inc. / Women in the World Foundation (womenintheworld.org/solutions/entry/womens-shelter-inc)*

- *Shelters for Women (www.ask.com/Shelters For Women)*

Training Centers

- *Mormon church operates 14 missionary training centers around the world (www.deseretnews.com/Mormon-church-operates-14-mis)*

- *History of the Missionary Training Center, locations around the world (www.deseretnews.com/%E2%80%A6/History-of-the-Missionary-Training)*

- *Training Centers: Navy Locations: About the Navy: Navy.com (http://www.navy.com/about/locations/training-centers.html)*

- *Condoray Women's Training Center–Saint Josemaria Escriva (www.josemariaescriva.info)*

- *Mormon school in Mexico to become a Missionary Training Center (http://www.sltrib.com/sltrib/opinion/51758464-82/church-latin-lds-missionaries.html.csp)*

- *Center for Women's Leadership Initiatives / 2011 / Press Releases (http://www.iie.org/)*

- *Center for Women's Leadership Initiatives / Centers of Excellence (http://www.iie.org/%E2%80%A6/Center-for-Women)*
- *Young Women From Around the Globe Get Leadership Training (http://www.georgetown.edu/)*
- *Training Institute / Events Around the World / Events / Get Involved (http://www.awid.org/)*
- *Defense Instr. Training (www.selfdefenseinstructortraining.com)*
- *International Women's Day (www.discov-her.com/Official)*

Counseling

- *Counseling Women–Women's Counseling Center (www.TerriPageTherapy.com)*
- *Find A Therapist / TherapyTribe.com (www.TherapyTribe.com)*
- *ProfessionalCounseling–LookingForProfessionalCounseling? (Local.com/Professional Counseling)*
- *Online Counseling Degrees / Counseling.EducationMatch.us (www.Counseling.EducationMatch.us)*
- *Counseling AROUND World–American Counseling Association (http://www.counseling.org/%E2%80%A6/78077-FM.PD)*
- *Behind the book: Counseling Around the World / Counseling Today (ct.counseling.org/2013/.../behind-the-book-counseling-around-the-world)*
- *Telephone counseling–Wikipedia, the free encyclopedia (en.wikipedia.org/wiki/Telephone counseling)*
- *Relationship counseling–Wikipedia, the free encyclopedia (en.wikipedia.org/wiki/Relationship counseling)*

- *American Association of Christian Counselors (www.aacc. net/about-us)*

- *College of Education and Social Services: University of Vermont (www.uvm.edu/cess/Page=facbio.php)*

- *Clinical Staff / Restoration Place Counseling (rpcounseling. org/who-we-are/staff)*

- *Domestic Violence: An Overview–Find Counseling.com (www. findcounseling.com)*

- *Do you require psychological counseling after you...–Women on Web*

Rights for Women

Women's Human Rights around the world is an important indicator to understanding global well-being. A major global women's rights treaty was ratified by the majority of the world's nations a few decades ago. Yet, despite many successes in empowering women, numerous issues still exist in all areas of life, ranging from the cultural and political to the economic. For example, women often work more than men, yet are paid less; gender discrimination affects girls and women throughout their lifetime; and women and girls are often the ones that suffer the most poverty.

Many may think that women's rights are only an issue in countries where religion is law, as in many Muslim countries. Or even worse, some may think this is no longer an issue at all. But reading this report about the United Nation's Women's Treaty and how an increasing number of countries are lodging reservations will show otherwise. Gender equality furthers the cause of child survival and development for all of society, so the importance of women's rights and gender equality should not be underestimated.

Related to Women's Shelters Around the World

- *Houses and homes around the world*
- *Famous women around the world*
- *Beautiful women around the world*
- *Women's health around the world*
- *Women's rights around the world*
- *Women's suffrage around the world*
- *Female Shelters*
- *Emergency Shelters*
- *Shelters in Chicago*
- *Women's Shelter*

International Women's Day

- *Holidays for Women*
- *International Women's Day–Time and Date*
- *www.timeanddate.com–Calendar–Holidays*
- *Calendar of Holidays and Events–English Club*
- *www.englishclub.com/vocabulary/calendar.htm*
- *Earth Calendar*
- *www.earthcalendar.net*
- *Guided Walking and Activity Holidays for Women, World-wide*
- *Walkingwomen.com*
- *World Denver–Blog*
- *www.worlddenver.org*

About the Author

FASHION IS LIKE art to me. Some people look at a particular piece of art, and it's like... they just don't get it. I see it as one of the most beautiful things in the world. I don't consider only the high class pieces to be fashionable and fabulous.

I think, as in most cases, beauty is in the eye of the beholder. A trend is a particular part of fashion that society is focusing on **at that moment**. Personal style is a woman's means of expressing herself through clothing, hair, and accessories. Know your style, like your favorite pair of shoes! Don't wait on the next new trend, be the next new trend.

Know who you are and who you should be. Find your gift and understand what it takes to master your gift. Have a clear vision of where you are and where you want to go. Know your flawless role based on your personal experiences, education, and career goals. Do what you love, own it, no matter who you are and live a fabulous lifestyle overall. "Do You!"

Bring joy to your soul, JOIN THE MOVEMENT. A Change for Lives! To heal and to celebrate a beautiful, recommitted, self-confident, "Fabulous, Healthy, Wealthy, and Think Like A New Boss Lifestyle."

Lauren Freeman will transform the lives of women by catering to their social, professional, and personal needs, providing solutions which transcend one time experience.

Lauren is on track and establishing herself as a highly respected and admired public figure.

Lauren and her family make their home in Plano, Texas.

"To be polished, it requires thinking, planning, simplifying and making tough choices. It may not be easy, but overall, it makes you look beautiful and actually makes life more fabulous!"

—Lauren Freeman

Why subscribe today? *To help Empower Your Life.*

- *Exclusive Content*
- *Stay Current*
- *Update Others*
- *Fashion Tips*
- *Health & Beauty Care Products*
- *Win a Closet Makeover*

Sign up at www.laurenfabulousfirm.com
5960 West Parker Road, Suite 278-120 Plano, Texas 75093

Founder and CEO of Lauren Fabulous Firm, LLC an organization dedicated to improving women's lifestyles, building a strong platform that helps women lead better lives. A firm that promotes Fabulous Women leaders, their images, beauty, careers, and lifestyles globally.

References

Source: Having good posture, http://www.everydayhealth.com/pain-management-pictures/6-ways-to-get-through-a-painful-workday.aspx#02

Source: Sitting posture, http://www.everydayhealth.com/health-center/sitting-info.aspx

Source: UK... dehydrated, http://www.patient.co.uk/doctor/acute-kidney-injury-pro

Source: Dress for Success, http://www.superseventies.com/info-bank/dress_for_success.html

Source: Glassdoor, http://www.glassdoor.com/Overview/Working-at—24-7-EI_IE34134.11,16.htm

References: Hockenbury, D., & Hockenbury, S. E. (2007). *Discovering Psychology.* New York, NY: Worth Publishers.

Myers, D. G. (1999). *Social Psychology.* McGraw-Hill College.

Smith, E. R. & Mackie, D. M. (2007). *Social Psychology.* London: Psychology Press.

Source: Martha Stewart, http://connection.ebscohost.com/c/articles/27047795/martha-comes-clean.

Source: http://www.glassdoor.com/Overview/Working-at—24-7-EI_IE34134.11,16.htm

CPSIA information can be obtained at www.ICGtesting.com
Printed in the USA
LVOW10s0027240816

501571LV00034B/614/P